Measuring transparency to improve good governance in the public pharmaceutical sector

Jordan

Regional Office for the Eastern Mediterranean

WHO Library Cataloguing in Publication Data

World Health Organization. Regional Office for the Eastern Mediterranean

Measuring transparency to improve good governance in the public pharmaceutical sector: Jordan / World Health Organization. Regional Office for the Eastern Mediterranean

p.

ISBN: 978-92-9021-649-0

1. Pharmaceutical Services - organization and administration - Jordan 2. Public Sector - Jordan 3. Drug Approval 4. Drug Evaluation I. Title II. Regional Office for the Eastern Mediterranean

(NLM Classification: QV 737)

© World Health Organization 2009

All rights reserved.

The designations employed and the presentation of the material in this publication do not imply the expression of any opinion whatsoever on the part of the World Health Organization concerning the legal status of any country, territory, city or area or of its authorities, or concerning the delimitation of its frontiers or boundaries. Dotted lines on maps represent approximate border lines for which there may not yet be full agreement.

The mention of specific companies or of certain manufacturers' products does not imply that they are endorsed or recommended by the World Health Organization in preference to others of a similar nature that are not mentioned. Errors and omissions excepted, the names of proprietary products are distinguished by initial capital letters.

The World Health Organization does not warrant that the information contained in this publication is complete and correct and shall not be liable for any damages incurred as a result of its use.

Publications of the World Health Organization can be obtained from Distribution and Sales, World Health Organization, Regional Office for the Eastern Mediterranean, PO Box 7608, Nasr City, Cairo 11371, Egypt (tel: +202 2670 2535, fax: +202 2670 2492; email: DSA@emro.who.int). Requests for permission to reproduce WHO EMRO publications, in part or in whole, or to translate them – whether for sale or for noncommercial distribution – should be addressed to the Coordinator, Knowledge and Management and Sharing, at the above address; email HIT@emro.who.int).

Printed by WHO Regional Office for the Eastern Mediterranean Region

Contents

Foreword 5
Preface 7
Acknowledgements 8
Executive summary 9
1. Introduction 12
2. Overview of the public pharmaceutical sector in Jordan 14
   2.1 Country information 14
   2.2 Health system in Jordan 14
   2.3 Relevant pharmaceutical organizations 15
   2.4 Relevant regulations 16
   2.5 Pharmaceutical market 17
3. Methodology 18
   3.1 Study design 18
   3.2 Selection of key informants 18
   3.3 Conducting the interviews 19
   3.4 Data collecton and scoring 19
4. Results 21
   4.1 Summary 21
   4.2 Medicine registration 22
   4.3 Control of medicines promotion 28
   4.4 Inspections 33
   4.5 Selection 37
   4.6 Procurement 41
   4.7 Distribution 46
5. Data analysis and interpretation 51
   5.1 Summary 51
   5.2 Medicine registration 52
   5.3 Control of medicine promotion 52
   5.4 Inspections 53
   5.5 Selection 53
   5.6 Procurement 54
   5.7 Distribution 54
6. Recommendations 56
7. Conclusions 60

Annexes
1. Scores for sections 61
2. Ministry of Health organizational chart.. 65
3. Jordan Food and Drug Administration organizational chart 66
4. Joint Procurement Department organizational chart... 67
5. List of evidence obtained.. 68

Foreword

Jordan has made great achievements in the provision of health services in recent years. The main indicators of the health status of Jordanian people are considered among the best in our region. In the pharmaceutical field, creation of the Jordan Food and Drug Administration in 2003 and Joint Procurement Department in 2004 have been milestones in the country's efforts towards more efficiency and transparency in medicines regulation and supply.

However, there are still important challenges facing health development in Jordan. Our main objective is to strengthen the response and performance in the national health system in order to achieve better health, equity in access to health care and a responsive health system that rises to the expectations of the people in Jordan.

The Government of Jordan considers the pharmaceutical sector as a crucial part of the health system, and is fully committed to continuously assessing and identifying areas for improvement in its structure and function. As part of this quest for excellence the Jordan Food and Drug Administration, in collaboration with the Ministry of Health and WHO, conducted this transparency study using a standard tool developed by WHO: "Measuring transparency to improve good governance in the public pharmaceutical sector" in December 2007. The aim was to provide a comprehensive picture of the level of transparency and vulnerability to corruption in six essential functions of the public pharmaceutical system, i.e. registration, promotion, inspection, selection, procurement and distribution of medicines.

The results of this study represent the views of a wide range of knowledgeable professionals who are well aware of the pharmaceutical situation in Jordan. Acknowledging this, the Ministry of Health and the Jordan Food and Drug Administration have taken the results into serious consideration. In February 2008, at the national workshop for disseminating and discussing the results, we committed to addressing the gaps identified in this important assessment. This commitment extends beyond improving the specific areas identified in this assessment. Transparency and accountability are important pillars of good governance and it is our firm commitment to institutionalize these concepts in every sphere of medicine policy and management practice.

Our association with the World Health Organization is long-standing and it is also our partner in this important programme. I welcome this new publication and I am confident it will provide an important roadmap for promoting good governance in our pharmaceutical sector so that it can effectively deliver public goods to the public and achieve its other development objectives.

Professor Salah Mawajdeh
Minister of Health
Jordan

Preface

The goal of the WHO Good Governance for Medicines programme is to improve the situation of medicines regulation and supply. Guided by the WHO Medicines Strategy and launched in late 2004, the programme is raising awareness of potential abuse in the public pharmaceutical sector and promoting good governance. Its ultimate aim is to ensure that essential medicines reach the people who need them, not the black market.

The World Bank has identified corruption as the single greatest obstacle to economic and social development. As the Good Governance project increases in momentum, more and more public health ministers and national medicines regulatory authorities are taking up the challenge to address it.

The Good Governance for Medicines programme offers a three-step technical support package which involves: national transparency assessment; development of a national framework on good governance for medicines; and implementation of a national programme. The global programme is being successfully implemented in some 30 countries around the world.

This report presents the findings of the first phase of the national Good Governance for Medicines programme in Jordan. The assessment aims to obtain a picture of the level of transparency and potential vulnerability to corruption in the public pharmaceutical sector using WHO's assessment instrument. In Jordan, the assessment looked at six functions: medicines registration, inspection of pharmaceutical establishments, promotion, selection, procurement and distribution.

The national assessment represents a baseline from which to monitor the country's progress over time in terms of transparency. However, by dealing with unethical practices, concepts of transparency and accountability, the assessment raises sensitive issues and it is imperative that it should be conducted in a constructive manner. The goal of the project is not to measure corruption but to examine how resistant or vulnerable the system is towards unethical practices.

The assessment is an entry point for the development and promotion of a national programme on good governance for medicines and should not be seen as an end in itself. It is the beginning of a process aimed at bringing about desirable and sustainable changes in the governance of the pharmaceutical sector. This exciting challenge has already been accepted by an increasing number of countries.

Assessment findings will help a country to identify vulnerable aspects that could lead to corruption and unethical practices. They will also determine what can be done to increase system transparency and accountability with the goal of improving access to medicines for peoples, especially vulnerable and marginalized groups.

Acknowledgements

This report was prepared by Adi Nuseirat, Head of the Rational Drug Use Department, Jordan Food and Drug Administration (JFDA). Dr Laila Jarrar, Drug Directorate Director, JFDA, reviewed the report and provided support. Dr Wael Inmair, coassessor for the study, collected and analysed the data. The views in this document were collected through interviews with a wide range of key informants whose experience and knowledge within the pharmaceutical sector in Jordan provided the basis for this assessment and its recommendations. WHO acknowledges the input of all contributors with thanks.

WHO also acknowledges with appreciation the support of HE Dr Salah Mawajdeh, Minister of Health and HE Dr Mohamed Rawashdeh, Director-General of the Jordan Food and Drug Administration. Their commitment to improving access to medicines in Jordan is indispensable to the initiation and continuation of efforts to curb corruption and increase transparency and accountability in the regulation and supply of medicines. The Ministry of Health provided additional information and support during the assessment process.

WHO is grateful to the Federal Ministry for Economic Cooperation and Development (BMZ), Germany, and the Department for International Development (DFID), United Kingdom, for their generous contribution to this work. The study would not have been possible without these sources of financial support.

Guitelle Baghdadi-Sabeti, of WHO headquarters, Zafar Mirza and Mohamed Ramzy, of WHO Regional Office for the Eastern Mediterranean, and Hashim ElZein El-Mousaad and Sana Naffa of WHO Jordan provided support to initiate the Good Governance for Medicines programme in Jordan and technical support throughout the assessment process.

Executive summary

This report presents the results of transparency assessments carried out in Jordan. It provides a comprehensive picture of the level of transparency and the potential vulnerability to corruption of six essential functions of the public pharmaceutical sector – registration, promotion, inspection, selection, procurement and distribution of medicines.

The methodology provides both qualitative and quantitative information. Two national investigators nominated from the Jordan Food and Drug Administration (JFDA) and from the Ministry of Health (national assessor plus co-assessor) collected data by conducting a series of interviews with carefully selected key informants. The information collected was then converted using a rough quantification method into a zero to 10 scale, to provide a score for each function in terms of vulnerability to corruption (minimal to extreme). The scoring indicates vulnerability in terms of the policy, the regulatory and administrative structures and the procedures at the time of the survey.

The quantitative data reveal that the areas of medicine distribution and procurement received the highest scores and are minimally vulnerable to corruption; medicines registration and selection are marginally vulnerable to corruption; medicine inspection is moderately vulnerable to corruption; while, medicine promotion had the lowest score and is extremely vulnerable to corruption.

Medicine registration

The area of medicine registration is well documented and the requirements for the registration of new medicines are fairly well standardized. There is fair access to information. The procedures for applicants on how to submit an application for registration of medicinal products are clearly written and publicly accessible. The principle weaknesses in the area of medicine registration are that there are no written guidelines on issues of conflict of interest, and members of registration committees are not required to declare any issues of conflict of interest; there are no clear and publicly accessible written procedures for assessors on how to assess submitted medicinal products for registration; and the criteria for selecting the members of the registration committees are not clear sufficiently to the public.

Control of medicine promotion

The provision in the medicines legislation does not cover all the activities regarding medicine promotion. Pre-approval of promotional and advertising materials for health providers is not officially required. The provision does not foresee an enforcement mechanism on promotion and advertisement of medicines, and the law does not state that sanctions or penalties should be applied for breaching the law. There is no formal complaints procedure to report unethical promotional practices. There is no government service or committee responsible for medicine promotion. The positive initiative in this area is that JFDA will soon launch guidelines to control medicine promotion activities.

Inspections

Although there is a comprehensive provision in the medicines legislation covering the inspection of medicine manufacturers and distributors, and there are written standard operating procedures for inspectors on how to conduct inspection, there are no written guidelines on conflict of interest with regard to inspection activities. There are no clear written criteria for selection and recruitment of inspectors. There are no written procedures to prevent regulatory capture between inspectors and the companies inspected and no external auditing of the inspection is done by inspectors from other countries.

Selection

In 2006, the government officially adopted a national essential medicines list, the Jordan Rational Drug List, which is available through the public health system, and helps the government to purchase appropriate medicines for their population. The government has clear guidelines that specify what criteria are applied for medicines to be included in or deleted from the rational drug list. The list is available in a printed format and available on the website of the JFDA[1]. A selection committee is appointed to give technical advice on the revision and update of the list. It includes physicians of different specializations and pharmacists. This area's principle weaknesses are that there are no written guidelines on conflict of interest regarding the selection of rational drugs; the criteria for selecting committee members are not made publicly available; the committee membership only includes experts from medicine and pharmacy field; the criteria do not require committee members to declare any conflict of interest issues; and, membership is not time-limited.

---

[1] See: http://jfda.jo/RDU/en-US/IndexPage.aspx (accessed 5 January 2009).

Procurement

Procurement of pharmaceuticals in public health obtained the highest rating of all six areas, thereby highlighting the high levels of transparency that characterize the procedures of this area, and indicating a minimal vulnerability to corruption. There are written guidelines for procurement office staff on the type of procurement method to be used for different types of products, and the procurement method chosen for each product aims to obtain the lowest possible purchase price for assured quality products. A formal appeals process is available for applicants who have their bids rejected. There are clear and specific criteria for tender committee membership. There are SOPs for routine inspection of consignments and the procurement office undergoes regular external auditing through the Audit Bureau. This area's principle weaknesses are that there are no written guidelines on conflict of interest with regard to the procurement process and the criteria for tender committee membership do not require that each member declare any conflict of interest issues. Also, not all procured medicines are from the national essential medicines list.

Distribution

The government has a transparent and explicit procedure that describes the distribution process for pharmaceutical products. The government medicines can be identified by imprints on containers and external packaging. There is systematic and orderly shelving of products in warehouses. There are inventory records and procedures in the warehouse at various levels of the distributing system. The warehouses are subjected to internal and external auditing. A computerized system provides information on medicines that have left a warehouse to health facilities. Sanctions are imposed on individuals for theft or corrupt practices. This area's principle weaknesses are that there is no effective security management to oversee storage and distribution and no programme exists for monitoring and evaluating the performance of the medicine distribution system.

In summary, the diagnostic framework and methodology that this study introduces can help health specialists and government decision makers prioritize those areas in the pharmaceutical system, which need the highest investment and regulation. This framework, in turn, helps to ensure that investments in the pharmaceutical system are maximized and that access to essential medicines is improved.

1. Introduction

Medicines registration, selection, procurement, promotion, inspection and distribution are core functions of the pharmaceutical sector. The structures and processes involved in each of these functions must work optimally to ensure the availability of safe, effective and appropriate medicines of the required quantity and at reasonable cost.

Transparency means clarity, honesty and openness. It is the principle on which the duty of civil servants, managers and trustees to act visibly, predictably and understandably is based and that those affected by administrative decisions should be informed of the process and the decisions taken. Transparency thus encompasses access, relevance, quality and reliability, and describes the increased flow of timely and reliable economic, social and political information. It enables institutions and the public to make informed political decisions, it improves the accountability of governments, and reduces the scope for corruption. Transparency is also essential to the economy; it improves resource allocation, enhances efficiency and increases growth prospects. Lack of transparency in the pharmaceutical sector can waste resources, which in turn reduces the availability of essential medicines and so threatens the well-being of populations.

Transparency International defines corruption as: "the abuse of entrusted power for private gain". Efforts to address the issue of corruption in the public sector have focused on the application of two basic strategies. One strategy has been the legislative reform approach, which establishes laws against corruption with appropriate punitive consequences for violations. This approach is often referred to as the "discipline approach", which attempts to deter corrupt practices through the fear of punishment. The second strategy, often termed the "values approach", attempts to increase institutional integrity by promoting moral values and ethical principles as a way of motivating public servants to behave ethically. Experience with these two strategies has shown that neither is sufficient if used alone and coordinated use of both is required to have a significant impact on establishing ethical practices within an institution.

This report summarizes the findings of the national transparency assessment in the pharmaceutical public sector that was carried out in Jordan between October and December 2007. The aim of the study was to assess the vulnerability to corruption of the six decision points in the pharmaceutical sector, namely: registration of medicines, control of medicine promotion, inspection of establishments, selection of essential medicines, procurement of medicines, and distribution of medicines. This assessment is an initial step in the effort to increase the transparency and accountability of the pharmaceutical sector. Based on the results of the assessment, it will be followed by the development and implementation of a national officially adopted Good Governance of Medicine (GGM) programme in Jordan. At the time of writing this report, many departments had already taken steps to develop national ethical frameworks and to revise administrative procedures, implying that a new assessment would result in higher scores.

2. Overview of the public pharmaceutical sector in Jordan

2.1 Country information

Jordan's population[2] is 5.4 million (2005). Gross national income per capita[3] is US$ 2500 (2005). Among the population living below the poverty line[4] 2% live on less than US$ 1/day and 7% below US$ 2/day (2002–2003 expenditure-based estimates). The per capita expenditure on health in Jordan was US$ 177 in 2003[5]. Total expenditure as a percentage of gross domestic product was 9.4% in 2003 with one third of this expenditure spent on medicines.

The country is signatory to several major trade agreements which impact health. Jordan has been a member of the World Trade Organization since 11th April 2000. Examples of these agreements include: the Free Trade Agreement (FTA) with USA (17th December 2001); the Association agreement with EU (1st May 2002), which aims to create a FTA with EU by 2010; the FTA with European Free Trade Area (EFTA) States including Iceland, Liechtenstein, Norway and Switzerland (21st June 2001); and, the FTA with Singapore (16th May 2004). Many medicines, excluding antibiotics, are charged up to 5% as an import fee depending on the country & the trade agreements with Jordan.

2.2 Health system in Jordan

The Ministry of Health is the principal provider of health care and provides subsidized services to all Jordanian citizens. The Ministry of Health operates hospitals, comprehensive health centres, primary health centres, maternity and child health centres, dental clinics and chest disease centres to provide healthcare for citizens. It also administers the Civil Insurance Program, which is the largest public insurance mechanism in Jordan. The other providers of healthcare in Jordan include the Royal Medical Services, which provides medical services to the military and their dependants.

---

[2] World Bank 2006
[3] World Bank (Atlas method) 2005
[4] *World Development Report 2007: Development and the next generation.* Washington, World Bank, 2007.
[5] *World Health Report 2006: Working together for health.* Geneva, World Health Organization, 2006.

National or social health insurance coverage as percentage of total population[6] extends to 68% of the population while 32% remain un-insured. Some of the population have multiple insurance coverage. The National Institute for Health covers 55%, the Refugee's Mission covers 18%, and private insurance coverage reaches 8%.

2.3 Relevant pharmaceutical organizations

The Joint Procurement Department (JPD) was established in 2004 for joint procurement of medicines and medical devices for the public sector. In 2007, JPD started procurement of 142 items (anti-infectives). The plan for the next 2 years is to procure all the medicines for public sector.

The Jordan Food and Drug Administration (JFDA) was created in 2003 as the sole national competent authority for medicines safety and efficacy, and food safety and quality. It includes the Drug Directorate, which deals with the medicine from its early stages as a raw material up to a finished product ready to be used by the patient. The Drug Directorate is responsible for registering and pricing the medicine (according to approved guidelines set by the Prime Minister and published in the local newspapers). The Drug Directorate follows up on clinical studies and monitors them through all stages. It includes the monitoring and inspection department that follows up on the inspection of all pharmaceutical institutions. It also includes the narcotics department, which deals with monitoring narcotics and the issuance of licences for concerned parties. The exporting and importing departments also fall under the jurisdiction of the Drug Directorate. The Drug Directorate includes a quality control laboratory, which is considered as one of the most important entities for medicine quality assurance in Jordan. Finally the Drug Directorate is responsible for the rational use of medicines.

There are many working committees involved in all the sectors (public, private and academic) in the Drug Directorate (according to the Drug And Pharmacy Law[7]). Their main responsibility is to take the right decision concerning different issues. They include: the technical committee for the registration of new medicines (originators); pricing committee; studying the generic medicine committee; accreditation of pharmaceutical sites committee; studying the medicinal plants and herbs committee; studying the cosmetics committee; vitamins committee; vaccines and sera committee; medical devices committee; bioequivalence studies committee; clinical studies committee; and the re-registration of registered products committee.

---

[6] *Medicine prices availability affordability in Jordan*. Amsterdam, Health Action International, 2007. Available at: http://www.haiweb.org/medicineprices/surveys/200405JO/sdocs/survey-report.pdf (accessed 5 January 2009).
[7] Provisional law No. 80 of the year 2001. It will be referred to in the rest of the document as "Drug and Pharmacy Law". Available online at http://www.jfda.jo/EN/Laws/details.aspx?id=71 (accessed 5 January 2009).

2.4 Relevant regulations

- National Medicines Policy since 1998. Current version (2001) known as Provisional Law No. 80 Drug and Pharmacy Law for the year 2001. The law is under review and contains many articles relating to the medicine pricing process and regulation.

- Instructions for marketing of unregistered drugs that are imported in non-commercial quantities for specific named patients.

- Criteria of considering the drug having a therapeutic advantage

- Information and documents required from the licensor

- The approved countries at the Food and Drug Administration as an alternative to the free sale certificates for the purposes of implementing Article No. (6) of the criteria of drug registration.

- Pharmacovigilance directives

- Drug promotion control (2008)

- The criteria and standards related to drugs pricing, re-pricing and objections to pricing decisions

- Import and export requirements of the various vaccines and plasmas and its derivatives

- Arab guidelines on current good manufacturing practices (cGMP) for pharmaceutical products

- Narcotic drug and psychotropic substance law (regulations and instructions)

- Clinical research law (provisional law no. 97 for the year 2001, law of clinical studies)

- Patent Law 21 of 2001 is in force. In addition, the Unfair Competition and Trade Secrets Law 15 of 2000 provide considerable protection for pharmaceutical products. Under this law, the duration of data protection is for five years starting on the date of receiving marketing approval and covers products registered by foreign companies after the law became enacted, regardless of whether or not the product is still in-patent.

- Bolar-like provision exists—9 months before patent expiry, generic manufacturers can submit bioequivalence test results and start the market application procedure. However, if the product is protected by Data Protection filed under Law 15 of 2000, the JFDA does not accept any applications for regulatory approval.

2.5 Pharmaceutical market

There are sufficient numbers of manufacturers (17 local) and importers for generic price competition to occur. However, competition is not fully free since JFDA sets a maximum price ceiling for generics as 80% of innovator. Expenditure on pharmaceuticals[8] is 30% of total health expenditure with 17.4% of total health expenditure taking place at retail pharmacies.

---

[8] Jordan National Health Accounts 2001. Available at:
http://www.healthsystems2020.org/content/resource/detail/1812/ (accessed 5 January 2009).

3. Methodology

3.1 Study design

A set of questionnaires was compiled for each function of the assessment, where four methods were used to determine the level of transparency of the practice. The methodology used in this assessment is intended primarily to collect qualitative information on selected indicators and then quantify the vulnerability to corruption by having a final score (Method 1 and 2) and perceptions of relevant health professionals in the public and private sectors (Method 3). Method 4 is used to capture additional information by using open-ended questions. The instrument for measuring transparency in the public pharmaceutical sector was used. The instrument is available online.[9]

To implement the study, a national assessor (NA) was selected and cleared by the Ministry of Health based on WHO recommendations. The assessor managed the whole assessment exercise, receiving training on the use of the assessment methodology and accompanying tools, planning meetings with key informants, carrying out the interviews, compiling and analysing the results, and writing the report describing the findings of the assessment. A team of co-assessors was selected from different institutions and trained by WHO to provide necessary support to the national assessor.

3.2 Selection of key informants

The team interviewed 61 carefully selected key informants (KIs). They were selected based on their knowledge about the subject and/or their level of involvement in the pharmaceutical sector. The KIs were selected to include both senior and junior professionals. They included governmental officials, both former and present employees involved in: medicine registration, including registration department staff and registration committees; selection, including national pharmacy and therapeutic committee and representatives from governmental hospitals; procurement including staff of the procurement office and members of tender committees; promotion, including representatives from the rational drug use department; inspection, including

---

[9] See: http://www.who.int/medicines/areas/policy/goodgovernance/AssessmentinstrumentENG.pdf (accessed 5 January 2009).

Table 1. Distribution of KIs across government, private sector, academic, nongovernmental organization and former government employees

Section	Government	Private	Academic	NGO	Former government employee	Total
Registration	4	5	0	1	0	10
Promotion	1	5	3	1	0	10
Inspection	4	5	0	0	1	10
Selection	7	1	1	1	0	10
Procurement	8	1	1	0	1	11
Distribution	6	3	1	0	0	10
Total	30	20	6	3	2	61

staff of the inspection department; distribution, including staff of the central warehouse and pharmacists from governmental hospitals; as well as members of the private sector, including representatives from the local and international pharmaceutical industry, and, representatives from the academic sector and nongovernmental organizations (NGOs). Table 1 shows the distribution of the KIs across government, private sector, academic, nongovernment organizations and former governmental employees. The NGO sector was not represented to a highly visible extent as only a few of them are involved with public procedures.

3.3 Conducting the interviews

Both the national assessor and a co-assessor were present in interviews. KIs were assured that opinions were confidential. Interviews were conducted in the offices of KIs.

3.4 Data collection and scoring

During the two-month study period, data collection involved utilizing a diagnostic tool for interviewing a total of 61 key informants—10 per decision point, except for the procurement function where 11 KIs were interviewed. Each indicator required a "yes" or "no" response from the KIs determining the presence or absence of the existing practice at the department of health. On this basis, a "yes" answer is given a value of "1" and a "no" answer is given a value of "0" by the researcher. A value of "1" represents low vulnerability to corruption, while the value of "0" represents high vulnerability to corruption. The sum of all ratings is then divided by the number of indicators in a given key decision point and multiplied by 100% to get the total percentage for each section. The result (percentage) is multiplied by 10 to convert to a scale of zero to 10.

Table 2 shows the 10 point rating system representing the following degrees of vulnerability to corruption.

Table 2. Scale for degrees of vulnerability to corruption

0.0 – 2.0	2.1 – 4.0	4.1 – 6.0	6.1 – 8.0	8.1 – 10.0
Extremely vulnerable	Very vulnerable	Moderately vulnerable	Marginally vulnerable	Minimally vulnerable

4. Results

4.1 Summary

This section of the report presents results of the questionnaires, which were filled in by the national assessor and the co-assessor with the 61 key informants. It gives a narrative account of the KIs' answers for each indicator with some clarifications where necessary. A summary of the quantitative results of scoring is given in Annex 1.

The following section focuses on the qualitative results based on KI's answers and the evidence gathered throughout the study.

The overall scores for each function of the assessment are summarized in Table 3.

KIs were asked to give their opinion on a series of statements. The responses are reported in Table 4.

Table 3. Vulnerability scale scores in the six different sections

	Registration	Promotion	Inspection	Selection	Procurement	Distribution
Indicator 1	1*	0.9	1	1	0.928	1
Indicator 2	0.9375	0.4	0.825	---	1	---
Indicator 3	0.9571	0	0.5634	0.9204	1	1
Indicator 4	0.5566	0.2	0.3497	0.8465	1	1
Indicator 5	0.9875	0	0	1	1	1
Indicator 6	1	0	1	---	0.575	0.3749
Indicator 7	1	0	0.74	0.5308	0	1
Indicator 8	0.595	0	0.15	0	---	1
Indicator 9	0.6218	---	---	1	1	1
Indicator10	0	---	---	0.8682	1	0.9833
Indicator11	---	---	---	---	0.969	0.725
Indicator12	0.3707	---	---	---	0.977	0.0143
Indicator13	---	---	---		---	1
Total	9.0262	1.5	4.6281	6.1659	9.450	10.0975
Final score**	**7.52**	**1.88**	**5.79**	**7.71**	**8.59**	**8.41**
Degree of vulnerability	Marginally vulnerable	Extremely vulnerable	Moderately vulnerable	Marginally vulnerable	Minimally vulnerable	Minimally vulnerable

* The numbers represent the average per question. It is calculated only on valid responses and all Don't know (DK) and Not applicable (NA) answers are discarded.
** Final score: total average/number of indicators x 10

Table 4. KI perceptions on the transparency level of each function

Section	Statement	Perception of KIs
Registration	The members of the registration committee are systematically and objectively selected based on the written criteria in force in Jordan	50% Strongly Agree or Agree
	Gifts and other benefits given to the officials in charge of medicines registration have no influence at all on the final decision	40% Strongly Agree or Agree, 40% Strongly Disagree or Disagree
Promotion	The legal provisions on drug promotion have been developed in broad consultation with all interested parties	60% Not applicable, 30% strongly disagree or disagree
	Civil society/NGOs have a great influence on improving the control of drug promotion in Jordan	60% Strongly Agree or Agree
	The provisions on drug promotion are well respected in Jordan	50% Strongly Disagree or Disagree, 50% Undecided or Not applicable
Inspection	The integrity of the inspectors is not at all influenced by personal gains, such as bribes, gifts, etc	50% Strongly Agree or Agree
Selection	The national essential medicines list (EML) has been developed in consultation with the opinion of all interested parties and using evidence-base approach	70% Strongly Agree or Agree
	The committee responsible for the selection of the national EML is operating free from external influence	60% Agree
Procurement	The members of the tender committee are systematically selected based on specific criteria	55% Agree
	The procurement system in Jordan is operating in a totally transparent manner	82% Strongly Agree or Agree
Distribution	The port clearing is done smoothly and there is no need for bribery or gift giving to expedite the process	60% Agree
	There are very rarely leakages in the medicine distribution system	50% Agree, 50% Disagree

4.2 Medicine registration

Indicator I.1: Is there an up-to-date list of all registered pharmaceutical products available in the country?

There is an easily accessible, official, up-to-date list of pharmaceutical products approved for sale or distribution in Jordan. Drugs not on the official list are non-approved and should not be available in the market for sale or use. Drug registration is based on an objective assessment of a drug's efficacy, safety, quality and the accuracy of the information on the product packaging.

Indicator I.2: If such a list exists, does it provide a minimum level of information?

The list provides sufficient and accurate information, and includes the description of the product including the name of the product, dosage form, strength, packaging, name of manufacturer, country of manufacture, site of manufacture, date of registration, registration number, validity of registration, and whether the medicine is prescription-only, or can be bought over-the counter (OTC).

Indicator I.3: Are there written procedures for applicants on how to submit an application for registration of medicinal products?

The written procedures for applicants on how to submit an application for registration of medicinal product are clear and published in the official gazette and on the JFDA website. They describe the process to follow for submitting an application, the data to be submitted, the timeframe for processing an application (less than 6 months), the fees, and the criteria for drug registration.

Indicator I.4: Are there written procedures for assessors on how to assess applications submitted for registration of medicinal products?

There are written procedures that describe the process to be followed in assessing submitted applications, which mention the time frame for processing and specify the issues to be considered in assessing submissions. However these procedures are not publicly accessible and do not provide guidance on report writing.

Indicator I.5: Is there a standard application form publicly available for the submission of applications for registration of medicinal products?

There is a standard application form made publicly available for the submission of applications for the registration of medicinal products. This document is available on the JFDA website[10] and is readily available in the JFDA office. It requires a description of the product, such as the name of the product (brand name and International Non-proprietary Name INN) and the composition per unit dose. It includes a brief summary of the manufacturing method; the specifications of pharmaceutical ingredients and excipients; the Summary of Product Characteristics (SPC), including the pharmacological action, therapeutic classification, indications and contraindications; and details of the packaging material and labelling.

Indicator I.6: Are there written guidelines setting limits on how and where medicine registration officers meet with applicants?

There are written guidelines for setting limits on where medicines registration officers meet the applicants, which state specific offices inside the JFDA building for such meetings. However, the guidelines don't include the number of registration officers present, to avoid any real or perceived conflict of interest in the outcomes of the meetings (usually one officer meets the applicant); and there are no minutes of the meetings that include the names of those in attendance, from either the applicant's or the Medicines Regulatory Authority (MRA) side.

Indicator I.7: Is there a functioning formal committee responsible for assessing applications for registration of pharmaceutical products?

---

[10] http://www.jfda.jo/en/Forms/details.aspx?id=48 (accessed 5 January 2009).

There are functioning formal committees responsible for assessing applications for registration of pharmaceutical products according to the Drug and Pharmacy Law[11] to ensure that the applications submitted for registration are assessed for efficacy, safety, quality, accuracy and completeness of product information. These committees are: the technical committee for the registration of new medicines (originators); the studying the generic medicine committee; the studying the medicinal plants and herbs committee; the vitamins committee; the vaccines and sera committee; the bioequivalence studies committee; and the re-registration of registered products committee.

Indicator I.8: Are there clear written criteria for selecting the members of the committee?

There are written criteria for selecting the members of two of the registration committees according to the Drug and Pharmacy Law[12] (technical committee for the registration of originators and generic medicine committee). It specifies the professional qualifications required, the required research experience in the area of expertise and gives a time-frame for serving as a committee member. It also specifies the technical skills and work experience related to the area and organizational affiliation to be considered when selecting members. However, it does not require declaration of conflict of interest (e.g. investment in a pharmaceutical company, spouse working in a pharmaceutical company, payment received from companies or individuals, etc.). The other registration committees, the studying the medicinal plants and herbs committee, the vitamins committee, and the vaccines and sera committee, do not have clear written criteria for selecting their members.

Indicator I.9: Is there a written document that describes the composition and terms of reference of the committee?

Technical committees have a written and publicly accessible document, available as part of the drug and pharmacy law, which describes the committee membership, roles and responsibilities. However, the committees do not include the accountability of the members.

Indicator I.10: Are there written guidelines on conflict of interest with regard to registration activities?

There are no written guidelines on conflict of interest and a conflict of interest declaration form does not exist with regard to registration activities.

Indicator I.11: To what extent do you agree with the following statement: "The members of the registration committee are systematically and objectively selected

---

[11] Articles 9,10
[12] Articles 9,10

based on the written criteria in force in your country"? (see question I.8)

50% agreed or strongly agreed with the statement "The members of the registration committee are systemically and objectively selected based on the written criteria in force in Jordan" (Table 5, Figure 1).

Indicator I.12: Are there clear and comprehensive guidelines for the committee's decision-making process?

Two of the registration committees, the technical committee for the registration of originators and the generic drug committee, according to the Drug and Pharmacy Law, have clear and comprehensive guidelines for their decision-making processes, and these are publicly available[13]. They specify the number of meetings that the committee should convene, the procedures for reaching decisions and the committee's reporting structure. The other technical committees do not have clear guidelines for their decision-making process.

Table 5. KI perceptions on membership selection for registration committee

Sector	Strongly disagree	Disagree	Undecided	Agree	Strongly agree	NA	DK	Total
Government	0	0	1	2	1	0	0	4
Private	0	1	1	2	0	1	0	5
NGO	0	0	1	0	0	0	0	1
Total	0	1	3	4	1	1	0	10

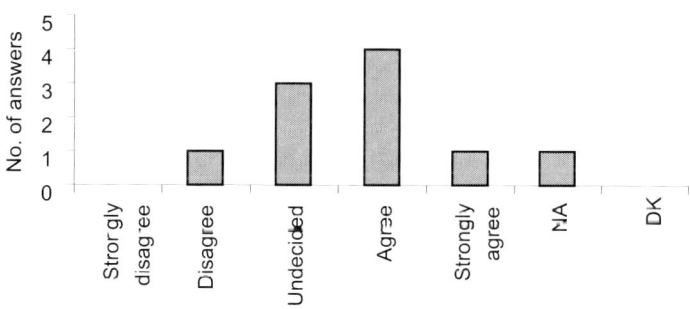

NA= not applicable; DK= do not know

Figure 1. Range of perceptions of KIs

---

[13] See: http://www.jfda.jo/EN/Laws/details.aspx?id=71

Indicator I.13: Is there a formal appeals system for applicants who have their drug applications rejected?

There is an appeal mechanism to manage concerns and complaints from companies and drug stores.

Indicator I.14: To what extent do you agree with the following statement: "Gifts and other benefits given to the officials in charge of medicines registration have no influence at all on their final decisions"?

40% agreed or strongly agreed with the statement "Gifts and other benefits given to the officials in charge of medicines registration have no influence at all on their final decisions" (Table 6, Figure 2).

Table 6. KI perceptions on officials in charge of medicines registration

Sector	Strongly disagree	Disagree	Undecided	Agree	Strongly agree	NA	DK	Total
Government	0	1	1	1	1	0	0	4
Private	1	1	0	2	0	0	1	5
NGO	0	1	0	0	0	0	0	1
Total	1	3	1	3	1	0	1	10

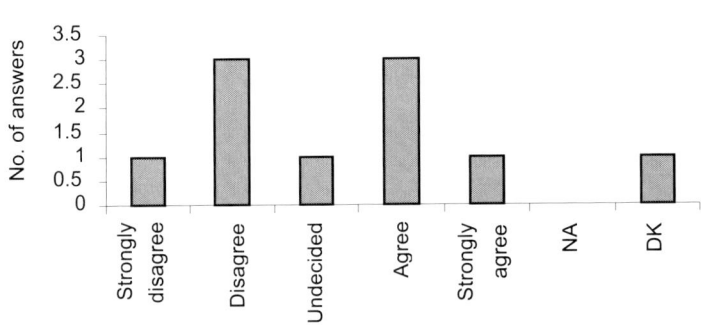

NA= not applicable; DK= do not know

Figure 2. Range of perceptions of KIs

Indicator I.15: In your opinion, what types of unethical behaviour are common in the registration system in your country? These can include bribery, material gifts, favouritism (family, friends), conflict of interest (e.g. investments in pharmaceutical companies), etc.

The common types of unethical behaviour in the registration system in Jordan:
- conflict of interest (3)
- favouritism (3)
- material gifts (2)

Indicator I.16: If you were in a position of highest authority, what would be the first actions that you would take to improve the registration process in your country?

a) The first actions that the KIs would take to improve the registration process in Jordan regarding the quality of services offered by public institutions would be to:

- Train employees of the public institution.
- Recruit qualified personnel.
- Build the experience of the staff and form in-house committees. The members of technical committees must be from registration staff. There is no need to have members from outside the JFDA.
- Adopt the support of external experts in the field of assessment.
- Follow and comply totally with the European guidelines regarding the documents needed for registration.
- Enhance the registration process by increasing the number of committee members.
- Increase the number of registration employees and increase the number of pharmacists allowed to receive applications, thus facilitating and accelerating the process of appointments.
- Adopt the international procedures for registration.
- Decrease the technical requirements for registration/re-registration of products (this was an opinion from private sector).

b) The first actions that the KIs would take to improve the registration process in Jordan regarding transparency in the services offered by public institutions would be to:

- Publish all requirements, processes and procedures.
- Publish SOPs.

- Increase the services provided on the JFDA website and increase the publicity of the website.
- Increase knowledge of the services offered and the way in which people work in order to increase awareness.
- Clarify the procedures of registration to the public.
- Enable submission of files on the website.
- Provide guidelines on conflict of interest and rules for the acceptance of gifts.
- Ensure that the appeal committee is different from the registration committee.
- Make sure that the manufacturer or the agent is in direct contact with the pharmacist who accepts/refuses the file.
- Accept applications electronically, particularly changes that occurred to the product.
- Ensure that the committees responsible for registration of medicines declare any conflict of interest issues.

4.3 Control of medicines promotion

Indicator II.1: Is there a provision in the medicines legislation/regulations covering medicine promotion and advertising?

There is a provision within the Drug and Pharmacy Law (article 35, 36 and 53) regarding promotion and advertising of medicines, but it does not cover all the activities regarding medicine promotion. However, more recently the JFDA is in the process of developing new regulations covering all medicine promotion activities.

Indicator II.2: Do the provisions on medicine promotion and advertising include explicit mention of the following areas?

The provisions on promotion of medicines mention the following areas: advertisement to professionals; advertisement to the public; qualification and training of medical representatives; restrictions on and monitoring of free samples; and packaging, labelling and package inserts. However, it does not cover symposia and scientific meetings; post-marketing scientific studies; speaker's fees and consultancies; promotion of exported medicines; and restrictions and limits on gifts and gimmicks.

Indicator II.3: Is pre-approval of promotional and advertising materials officially required?

Pre-approval of promotional and advertising materials for health providers is not officially required. Advertising materials are made available in the market without monitoring.

Indicator II.4: Do the provisions foresee an enforcement mechanism on the promotion and advertisement of medicines?

The provisions do not foresee an enforcement mechanism on the promotion and advertisement of medicines, and the law does not indicate the type of sanctions or penalties to be applied to public officials or pharmaceutical companies who are in breach of the law.

Indicator II.5: Is there a formal complaints procedure to report unethical promotional practices?

There is no formal complaints procedure to report unethical promotional practices.

Indicator II.6: Is there a service or committee responsible for monitoring and enforcing the provisions on medicine promotion?

There is no government service or committee responsible for monitoring and enforcing the provisions on medicine promotion.

Indicator II.7: Are there written and publicly available SOPs, guiding those responsible for pre-approving or monitoring medicine promotion and advertising?

There are no written SOPs guiding those responsible for pre-approving or monitoring medicine promotion and advertising.

Indicator II.8: Are there written guidelines on conflict of interest with regards to the control of medicine promotion activities?

There are no written guidelines on conflict of interest with regards to the control of medicine promotion activities.

Indicator II.9: To what extent do you agree with the following statement: "The legal provisions on medicine promotion have been developed in broad consultation with all interested parties"?

Nobody agreed with the statement: "The legal provisions on medicine promotion have been developed in broad consultation with all interested parties" (Table 7, Figure 3).

Table 7. KI perceptions on the legal provisions on drug promotion

Sector	Strongly disagree	Disagree	Undecided	Agree	Strongly agree	NA	DK	Total
Government	0	0	1	0	0	0	0	1
Private	2	1	0	0	0	2	0	5
Academic	0	0	0	0	0	3	0	3
NGO	0	0	0	0	0	1	0	1
Total	2	1	1	0	0	6	0	10

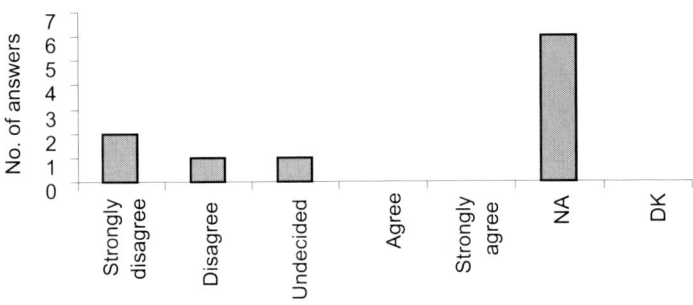

NA=not applicable; DK= do not know

Figure 3. Range of perceptions of KIs

Indicator II.10: To what extent do you agree with the following statement: "Civil society/NGOs have a great deal of influence on improving the control of medicine promotion in your country"?

60% agreed or strongly agreed with the statement: "Civil society/NGOs have a great deal of influence on improving the control of medicine promotion in Jordan." The majority of respondents answered this question in light of the potentially important role that NGOs could play (section 5.2) (Table 8, Figure 4).

Table 8. KI perceptions on the influence of civil society/NGOs on the control of medicine promotion

Sector	Strongly disagree	Disagree	Undecided	Agree	Strongly agree	NA	DK	Total
Government	1	0	0	0	0	0	0	1
Private	0	0	1	1	1	2	0	5
Academic	0	0	0	2	1	0	0	3
NGO	0	0	0	1	0	0	0	1
Total	1	0	1	4	2	2	0	10

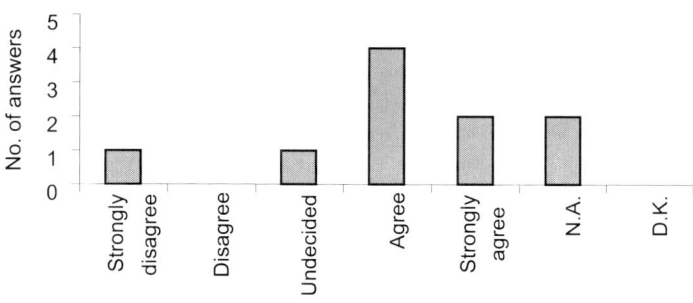

NA=not applicable; DK= do not know

Figure 4. Range of perceptions of KIs

Indicator II.11: To what extent do you agree with the following statement: "The provisions on drug promotion are well respected in your country"?

50% Strongly disagreed or disagreed with the statement: "The provisions on drug promotion are well respected in Jordan" (Table 9, Figure 5).

Table 9. KI perceptions on the provision of drug promotion control

Sector	Strongly disagree	Disagree	Undecided	Agree	Strongly agree	NA	DK	Total
Government	0	0	0	0	0	1	0	1
Private	2	1	0	0	0	2	0	5
Academic	0	1	2	0	0	0	0	3
NGO	0	1	0	0	0	0	0	1
Total	2	3	2	0	0	3	0	10

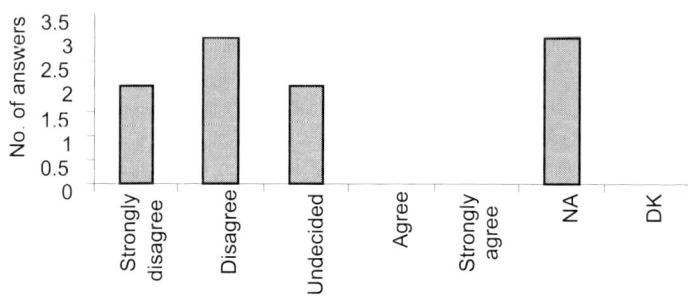

NA=not applicable; DK= do not know

Figure 5. Range of perceptions of KIs

Indicator II.12: In your opinion, what types of unethical behaviour are common in the drug promotion area in your country? These can include bribery, material gifts, favouritism (family, friends), conflict of interest (e.g. investments in pharmaceutical companies), etc.

a) Involving health professionals and health institutions in general.

The types of unethical behaviour that are common in the drug promotion area in Jordan regarding health professionals and health institutions in general:

- bribery (9)
- material gifts (9)
- favouritism (5)
- conflict of interest (2)

b) Involving regulatory office staff and committee members responsible for controlling drug promotion.

There is no regulatory office or any committee members responsible for drug promotion in Jordan.

Indicator II.13: If you were in a position of highest authority, what would be the first actions that you would take to improve the drug promotion process in your country?

a) The first actions that the KIs would take to improve the drug promotion process in Jordan in terms of the quality of services offered by public institutions would be to:

- Enforce legislation covering medicine promotion and advertising.
- Establish a committee/government service for monitoring and enforcing the provisions on medicine promotion.
- Write and make publicly available SOPs guiding the services responsible for pre-approving or monitoring medicine promotion.
- Monitor the action of the pharmaceutical companies during the process of promotion.
- Develop new regulations that would cover all medicine promotion-related issues.
- Introduce and enforce policies that establish and monitor ethical standards with respect to pharmaceutical company promotion to prescribers. The government should do this in collaboration with medical associations.
- Review and enforce laws and regulations to cover the complete control of medicine promotion.

- Ensure that medicine promotion is only permitted for the registered medicine and based on sound scientific studies.

- Train health professionals on how to adopt good prescribing practice.

- Enforce a law to monitor and punish any unethical practices of medicine companies.

- Introduce a comprehensive practitioner and consumer education programme about the impact of unethical medicine promotion.

b) The first actions that the KIs would take to improve the medicine promotion process in Jordan in terms of transparency of the services offered by public institutions would be to:

- Establish a committee responsible for controlling medicine promotion, with clear terms of reference, conflict of interest policies, and SOPs.

- Ensure clarity in the services offered by public institutions to the public and to health professionals.

- Publish all available regulations and guidelines concerning controlling medicine promotion.

4.4 Inspections

Indicator III.1: Is there a provision in the medicines legislation/regulation covering inspection of medicines manufacturers and distributors?

There is a provision in the medicines legislation covering inspection of medicines manufacturers and distributors (Drug and Pharmacy Law, articles 72 and 73).

Indicator III.2: Is the provision on inspection comprehensive enough?

The provision on inspection gives the inspectors power to inspect premises and activities. It gives the inspectors the power to enter, at any reasonable time, any place where medicinal products are produced, packaged, stored, distributed or tested in order to carry out an inspection. It defines the inspectors' duties, responsibilities and powers to take action in case of violations of provisions of the medicines legislation and or regulation and it requires inspectors to be provided with a special identification document. Finally, it requires that a copy of the provision is made available to companies being inspected.[14]

Indicator III.3: Are there written guidelines on classification of Good Manufacturing Practices (GMP) or Good Distribution Practices (GDP) non-compliance that describe

---

[14] Some of this is not applicable to the Jordanian inspectors who inspect manufacturers outside Jordan.

the types of deficiencies and the corresponding measures to be taken by the Medicines Regulatory Authority?

There are written guidelines on classification of GMPs[15]. The document is called "Arab Guidelines on Current Good Manufacturing Practices for Pharmaceutical Products." There are no written guidelines on the classification of GDPs. The GMP guidelines are available in writing and easily accessible to all stakeholders. The guidelines provide classification of GMP deficiencies, and the measures to be taken in case of non-compliance to it. However, there is no written appeals mechanism for companies, and if any company wishes to protest, the complaint will return back to the head of the inspection department or to the same inspector.

Indicator III.4: Are there written procedures/mechanisms to prevent regulatory capture between inspectors and the manufacturers or distributors that he/she inspects?

There are no written procedures to prevent regulatory capture between inspectors and the companies inspected. However the inspection department in Jordan have unwritten procedures that help to prevent regulatory capture between inspectors and manufacturers/distributors inspected. These include: rotation of inspectors based on a scheduling system; a rotation mechanism requiring inspectors from one geographical area to inspect companies in other areas; inspectors visit sites in teams with a team leader and inspect under the observation of another inspector who reports on what he/she has observed. There is no external auditing of the inspection done by inspectors from another country.

Indicator III.5: Are there written guidelines on conflict of interest with regards to inspection activities?

There are no written guidelines on conflict of interest with regards to inspection activities.

Indicator III.6: Are inspection findings and conclusions subject to an internal review?

The inspection findings and conclusions are subject to an internal review by the head of the inspection department.

Indicator III.7: Are there written SOPs for inspectors on how to conduct inspections?

Inspectors have written SOPs to guide them in performing their duties. These procedures are available in writing (to the inspectors) in the form of checklist. They detail the requirements for pre- and post-inspection activities, the scheduling system

---

[15] Available at: http://www.jfda.jo/EN/Laws/details.aspx?id=77 (accessed 5 January 2009).

that identifies companies due for inspections within a set timeframe, and the format and content of inspection reports. These SOPs are not made publicly available.

Indicator III.8: Are there written criteria for the selection and recruitment of inspectors?

The criteria for selection and recruitment of inspectors only include the professional qualifications required (pharmacist). Recruitment of inspectors does not require a minimum number of years of work experience in the area, and is not based on recommendations from former employers.

Indicator III.9: To what extent do you agree with the following statement: "The integrity of inspectors is not at all influenced by personal gains, such as bribes, gifts, material or other benefits, etc."?

50% agreed or strongly agreed with the statement "The integrity of inspectors is not at all influenced by personal gains, such as bribes, gifts, material or other benefits, etc." (Table 10, Figure 6).

Table 10. KI perceptions of the integrity of inspectors

Sector	Strongly disagree	Disagree	Undecided	Agree	Strongly agree	NA	DK	Total
Government	0	0	0	1	3	0	0	4
Private	1	2	2	0	0	0	0	5
Former government employee	0	0	0	1	0	0	0	1
Total	1	2	2	2	3	0	0	10

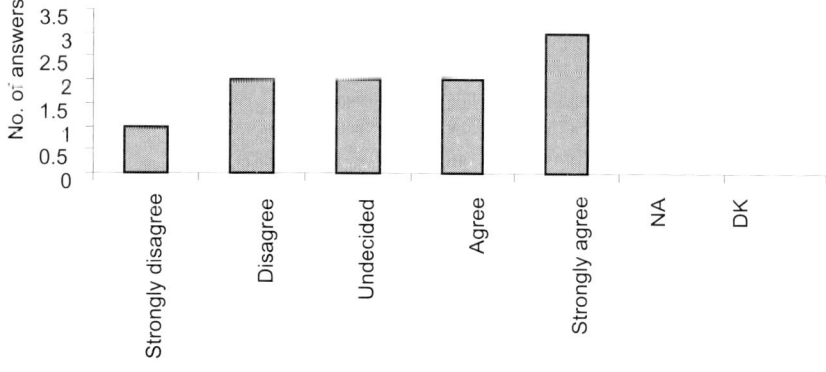

NA= not applicable; DK= do not know

Figure 6. Range of perceptions of KIs

Indicator III.10: In your opinion, what types of unethical behaviour are common in the inspection area in your country? These can include bribery, material gifts, favouritism (family, friends), conflicts of interest (e.g. investments in pharmaceutical companies), etc.

The common types of unethical behaviour in the inspection area in Jordan:

a) favouritism (4)
b) conflict of interest (1)
c) material gifts (1)

Indicator III.11: If you were in a position of highest authority, what would be the first actions that you would take to improve the inspection process in your country?

a) The first actions that the KIs would take to improve the inspection process in Jordan regarding the quality of inspection services offered by public institutions, would be to:

- Train the inspectors.
- Increase the salaries of inspectors.
- Increase the number of inspectors.
- Require clear and well-defined levels of qualification and experience for the recruitment of inspectors.
- Establish a clear rotation mechanism for inspectors.
- Stick to a pre-inspection plan through a checklist and a post-inspection report that should be submitted shortly after the inspection.
- Modify the pharmacy and medicine laws.
- Enforce clear guidelines to be followed.
- Introduce a pre-schedule visit timetable.
- Establish an independent directorate for inspection.
- Increase the significance of the role of the Assurance of Good Manufacturing Practice and Good Distribution Practice in medicine regulation.

b) The first actions that the KIs would take to improve the inspection process in Jordan regarding transparency in the services offered by public institutions would be to:

- Introduce an appeal system for companies.
- Require that pre-inspections be made in writing.

- Introduce written guidelines on conflict of interest with regard to inspection activities, as well as mechanisms for monitoring. Sanctions should be applied to those in breach of these guidelines.

- Introduce a system for a companies' inspection schedule.

- Publish all guidelines and procedures for inspection.

- Publish post inspection reports.

- Make the final report including all the inspectors' notes available to authorized personnel in the manufacturing plants upon request.

- Ensure that the conclusion of the inspection report is discussed with the company face to face.

- Ensure that the final report is signed by the company, the inspector's team, and the agent.

- Make all the regulation covering inspection of medicines, and all the guidelines and procedures regarding the inspection activity present on the website.

4.5 Selection

Indicator IV.1: Does the government have an officially adopted national essential medicines list (EML) publicly available?

The first essential medicines list was published in 1998, and updated in 2002. In 2006, the government officially adopted the Jordan Rational Drug List[16] (JRDL), which is available through the public health system, and helps the government to purchase appropriate drugs for their population.

Indicator IV.2: To what extent do you agree with the following statement: "The national essential medicines list has been developed in consultation with, and considering the opinion of, all interested parties and using an evidence-based approach"?

70% agreed or strongly agreed with the statement "The Jordan Rational Drug List has been developed in consultation with, and considering the opinion of, all interested parties and using an evidence-based approach" (Table 11, Figure 7).

---

[16] Jordan's Rational Drug List (JRDL) available at: http://www.jfda.jo/RDU/JNDFBook/Annex/Annex.htm (accessed 5 January 2009).

Table 11. KI perceptions of the JRDL

Sector	Strongly disagree	Disagree	Undecided	Agree	Strongly agree	NA	DK	Total
Government	0	0	2	2	3	0	0	7
Private	0	1	0	0	0	0	0	1
Academic	0	0	0	1	0	0	0	1
NGO	0	0	0	0	1	0	0	1
Total	0	1	2	3	4	0	0	10

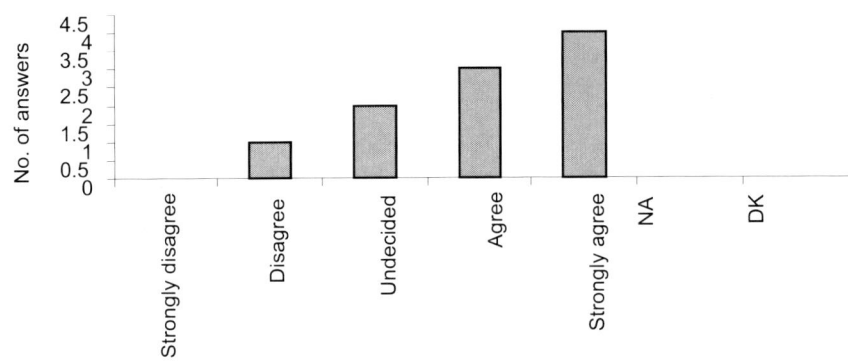

NA= not applicable; DK= do not know

Figure 7. Range of perceptions of KIs

Indicator IV.3: Are there clearly written and transparent rules/criteria for the selection process for including or deleting medicines from the national EML?

The government have clear guidelines that specify what criteria are applied for medicines to be included in or deleted from the JRDL[17]. The inclusion of new medicines should be based on studies that confirm that the medicine is necessary for the health needs of the population and is cost-effective, and the deletion of a drug from the JRDL is based on evidence that the drug is inappropriate or not cost-effective for the population's health needs. However, the committee of selection does not include a person who is experienced in pharmacoeconomics.

---

[17] For guidelines visit: http://www.jfda.jo/RDU/JNDFBook/Annex/Annex.htm

Indicator IV.4: Is the EML in line with WHO procedures?

The JRDL is available in a printed format and on the website of the JFDA[18] and is easily accessible by all health professionals. The products are listed by generic name, pharmacological category, and by level of health care. We do not have national treatment guidelines for all common diseases in Jordan, so the JRDL is not linked to national standard treatment guidelines, and the JRDL should be revised every 2 years.

Indicator IV.5: Is there a committee responsible for the selection of the national EML?

A selection committee is appointed to give technical advice on the revision and update of the JRDL. It includes physicians of different specializations and pharmacists.

Indicator IV.6: To what extent do you agree with the following statement: "The committee responsible for the selection of the national EML is operating free from external influence"?

60% agreed with the statement "The committee responsible for the selection of the national EML (JRDL) is operating free from external influence" (Table 12, Figure 8).

Table 12. KI perceptions of the selection of medicines on the JRDL

Sector	Strongly disagree	Disagree	Undecided	Agree	Strongly agree	NA	DK	Total
Government	0	1	2	4	0	0	0	7
Private	0	1	0	0	0	0	0	1
Academic	0	0	0	1	0	0	0	1
NGO	0	0	0	1	0	0	0	1
Total	0	2	2	6	0	0	0	10

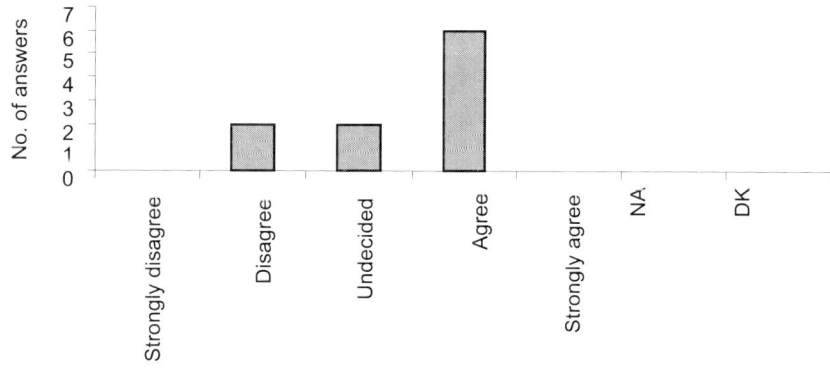

NA= not applicable; DK= do not know

Figure 8. Range of perceptions of KIs

---

[18] See: http://www.jfda.jo/RDL2/Annex/Annex.htm (accessed 5 January 2009)

Indicator IV.7: Are there clear criteria for the selection of members of the selection committee?

The criteria for selecting committee members are not made publicly available. However, the criteria define the professional requirements, and the committee only includes experts from the medicine and pharmacy fields. The criteria do not require declaration of conflict of interest, and membership is not time-limited.

Indicator IV.8: Are there written guidelines on conflict of interest with regard to the selection of essential medicines?

There are no written guidelines on conflict of interest and a conflict of interest declaration form does not exist.

Indicator IV.9: Are there clear and publicly available SOPs that describe the role and responsibilities of the selection committee?

There are clear and publicly available SOPs that describe the rules for the decision-making process. Decision is made by majority of the members. If the number of members who accept adding or selecting the medicine equal the number of the members who refuse it , the decision of the chairperson of the committee is considered.

Indicator IV.10: Are the rules for decision-making clear and transparent in the SOPs?

The rules for decision-making defined in the SOPs require that: decisions are made by all members in a democratic manner; minutes of meetings are produced and approved by the members; consultations are held with interested parties; final decisions for selecting medicines are taken independently; decisions on the selection process are made publicly available; and, minutes of meetings are disseminated publicly on the JFDA website.

Indicator IV.11: In your opinion, what types of unethical behaviour are common in the selection process in your country? These can include bribery, material gifts, favouritism (family, friends), conflicts of interest (e.g. investments in pharmaceutical companies), pressure on consultants by companies, etc.

The common types of unethical behaviour in the selection process in Jordan:

- material gifts (4)
- favouritism (3)
- conflict of interest (1)

Indicator IV.12: If you were in a position of highest authority, what would be the first actions that you would take to improve medicine selection?

a) The first actions that the KIs would take to improve medicine selection in terms of the quality of services offered by public institutions would be to:

- Ensure that choosing a medicine is dependant on cost-effectiveness studies.
- Publish the national standard treatment guidelines and ensure that they are linked to the rational medicine list.
- Ensure medicine selection is based on the scientific (generic) name.
- Set treatment guidelines for chronic diseases and ensure that doctors to stick to it
- Ensure that the selection committee must include a qualified member with a PhD in pharmacoeconomics.
- Make membership of the selection committee limited in time.
- Ensure a member from private sector is present on the selection committee.

b) The first actions that the KIs would take to improve medicine selection in terms of transparency in the services offered by public institutions would be to:

- Publish all the scientific information for the reasons of choosing these medicines.
- Set written guidelines on conflict of interest.
- Change the committees of selection every year.
- Train members to review on a cost-effectiveness basis.
- Set laws to force all doctors in the public sector to stick to the list.
- Ensure the rules for decision-making in the SOPs are clear and transparent to the public.

4.6   Procurement

Indicator V.1: Does the government use transparent and explicit procedures for procurement of pharmaceutical products?

The government has an explicit document that describes the procurement process for pharmaceutical products under the Joint Procurement Law of Medicines and Medical Supplies (2002)[19]. This document is publicly available and requires: the use of generic names; the advertisement of tenders; that contract specification is made publicly available; criteria for adjudication of tenders are included as part of the tender package; information on the tender process and results are made public; and a description of the internal process to be followed by the procurement staff on how to

---

[19] See: http://www.jpd.gov.jo/ReadPaner.php?id=110&sub_id=5 (accessed 5 January 2009)

process the bids. However, although the document requires procurement that is based on the Jordan Rational Drug List only the joint procurement directorate stick to it fully, and the other entities of the public sector only stick to 80%–90% of it.

Indicator V.2: Is there written guidance for procurement office staff on the type of procurement method to be used for different types of products?

There are several types of procurement methods used to purchase pharmaceutical products, which fall into one of four basic categories: open tender, restricted tender, competitive negotiations and direct procurement. The procurement method chosen for each product aims to obtain the lowest possible purchase price for assured quality products. Written guidance is available for procurement office staff on what procurement method to use for the different types of products to be purchased.

Indicator V.3: Is procurement done with an objective quantification method to determine the quantity of pharmaceuticals to be purchased?

Medicine procurement is based on objective, expected health needs, and on budget availability to reduce the risk of over-supply, under-supply, or unnecessary supply of pharmaceuticals.

Indicator V.4: Is there a formal appeals process for applicants who have their bids rejected?

An appeal mechanism works in the following way: If a firm is unsuccessful in its bid for a tender, a representative from the firm can file a protest based on the firm's view that the tender excludes it unfairly or that the tender process was flawed. This appeal process is available online[20].

Indicator V.5: Is there a tender committee? If so are the key functions of the procurement office and those of the tender committee clearly separated?

A tender committee is available. Its main role is to review information on suppliers and determine which suppliers should participate in the tender, if a restricted tender is used, and which suppliers should receive contracts. Staff from the procurement office, whose main role is to collect information on needs, manage the tender process and monitor the supplier's performance.

Indicator V.6: Are there any specific criteria for tender committee membership?

The criteria that the government has for selecting tender committee members is written in an article of the Joint Procurement Law of Medicines and Medical Supply. It includes that the procurement committee should be composed of members who

---

[20] See: http://jpd.gov.jo/ReadPaner.php?id=132&sub_id=127 (accessed 5 January 2009).

are appointed for their professional expertise. The members should have skills that complement each other, including senior government officials in departments served by the procurement system, and representation from client facilities (governmental hospitals). The membership rotates periodically every 2 years and is renewable for one time. The criteria do not require that each member should declare conflict of interest. The criteria for committee membership are publicly available[21].

Indicator V.7: Are there written guidelines on conflict of interest with regard to the procurement process?

There are no written guidelines on conflict of interest with regard to the procurement process.

Indicator V.8: To what extent do you agree with the following statement: "The members of the tender committee are systematically selected based on specific criteria (see question V.6)"?

55% agreed with the statement "The members of the tender committee are systemically selected based on specific criteria" (Table 13, Figure 9).

Indicator V.9: Is there a computerized management information system used to report product problems in procurement?

The management information system is computerized and it includes product records, and monitors supplier and facility performance. It also records all quality assurance information for products purchased, and tracks the status for each order, including the quantities actually purchased compared with the original estimates made.

Indicator V.10: Are there SOPs for routine inspection of consignments?

In Jordan, each drug shipment should be physically inspected. This involves checking adherence to contract specifications. Additionally batch samples should be sent to quality control laboratories using random sampling for known suppliers and systematic sampling for new ones. All documents including inspection reports and laboratory testing results should be archived in the procurement office.

Indicator V.11: Is there an efficient post-tender system in place to monitor and report on supplier's performance to the tender committee?

---

[21] See: http://www.jpd.gov.jo/ReadPaner.php?id=110&sub_id=5 (accessed 5 January 2009)

Table 13. KI perceptions of the tender committee

Sector	Strongly disagree	Disagree	Undecided	Agree	Strongly agree	NA	DK	Total
Government	0	1	2	5	0	0	0	8
Private	0	0	1	0	0	0	0	1
Academic	0	0	1	0	0	0	0	1
Former government employee	0	0	0	1	0	0	0	1
Total	0	1	4	6	0	0	0	11

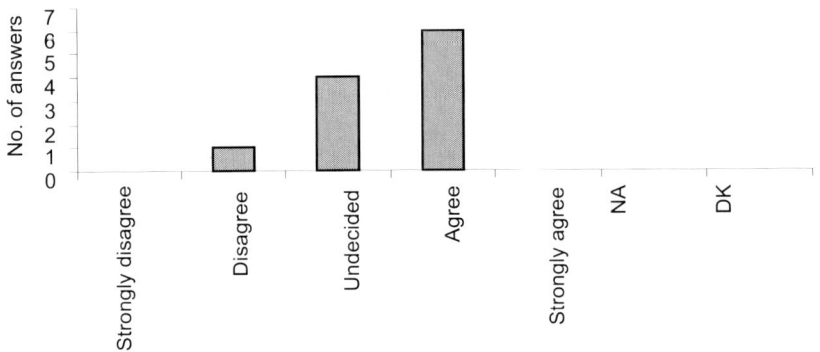

NA= not applicable; DK= do not know

Figure 9. Range of perceptions of KIs

The procurement office monitors supplier performance and compliance with the contract terms. The monitoring system tracks the supplier's lead-time, delivery status, shelf life, and packaging of products. Product quality is also tracked, and suppliers with poor performance are blacklisted for a certain period of time.

Indicator V.12: Does the procurement office undergo regular audits?

The procurement office should undergo external auditing through the Audit Bureau at least once a year, and its results are made publicly available in the Jordan Parliament council. The annual audit should report on the operating costs of the procurement office, pharmaceutical products tendered, quantities of the products procured, and the contracts awarded. Results of tenders are available online[22].

Indicator V.13: To what extent do you agree with the following statement: "The procurement system in your country is operating in a totally transparent manner"?

82% agreed or strongly agreed with the statement "The procurement system in Jordan is operating in a totally transparent manner" (Table 14, Figure 10).

---

[22] http://www.jpd.gov.jo/index_en.php (accessed 5 January 2009).

Table 14. KI perceptions of the procurement system

Sector	Strongly disagree	Disagree	Undecided	Agree	Strongly agree	NA	DK	Total
Government	0	0	1	4	3	0	0	8
Private	0	0	0	1	0	0	0	1
Academic	0	0	1	0	0	0	0	1
Former government employee	0	0	0	1	0	0	0	1
Total	0	0	2	6	3	0	0	11

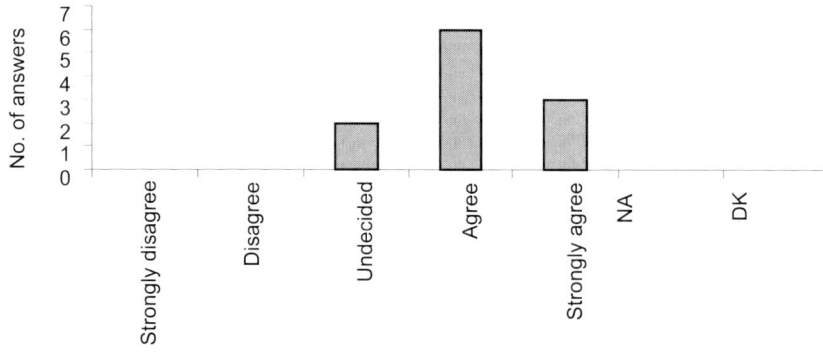

NA= not applicable; DK= do not know

Figure 10. Range of perceptions of KIs

Indicator V.14: In your opinion, what types of unethical behaviour are common in the procurement system in your country? These can include bribery, material gifts, favouritism (family, friends), conflict of interest (e.g. investments in pharmaceutical companies), etc.

The common types of unethical behaviour in the procurement system in Jordan:

a) material gifts (6)
b) bribery (3)
c) travelling (2)
d) favouritism (1)

Indicator V.15: If you were in a position of highest authority, what would be the first actions that you would take to improve the systems and processes of procurement?

a) The first actions that the KIs would take to improve the systems and processes of procurement in terms of the quality of procurement services would be to:

- Train employees of the public institution.

- Recruit qualified personnel.

- Re-structure the procurement department to include the following key functional areas: specification section; accountancy section; quality assurance section; including audit; procurement section; receiving and checking section; and information technology support.

- Make public sector tender procurement restricted to the JRDL.

- Review procedures to ensure that prospective suppliers are pre-qualified, and that their performance is monitored for product quality, service reliability, delivery time and financial viability, and appropriately recorded in a retrievable database.

- Simplify the procurement process to have a positive impact on the system and improve effectiveness. This could be achieved by: requiring a more evidence-based approach to medicine selection for procurement; and rationalization of medicine requirements, i.e. reducing the chemical entity in each therapeutic group, e.g. two beta blockers, two proton pump inhibitors.

b) The first actions that the KIs would take to improve the systems and processes of procurement in terms of transparency in procurement services would be to:

- Set written guidelines on conflict of interest with regard to the procurement process.

- Ensure that the submission of the tenders process can be done online on the website and that the results are posted on the website.

- Ensure that the members of the tender committee are required to declare any conflict of interest issues.

- Enforce the blacklisting of non-performing or poor performing suppliers. This should be regularly updated and a copy of the list forwarded to the procurement department.

4.7 Distribution

Indicator VI.1: Is there a system in place that can expedite port clearing?

The medical stores have a person that is responsible for port clearing and there is a computerized system to monitor port clearing activities.

Indicator VI.2: To what extent do you agree with the following statement: "Port clearing is done smoothly and there is no need for bribery or gift-giving to expedite the process"?

Table 15. KI perceptions of port clearing

Sector	Strongly disagree	Disagree	Undecided	Agree	Strongly agree	N.A.	D.K.	Total
Government	0	0	0	5	0	0	1	6
Private	0	0	2	1	0	0	0	3
Academic	0	1	0	0	0	0	0	1
Total	0	1	2	6	0	0	1	10

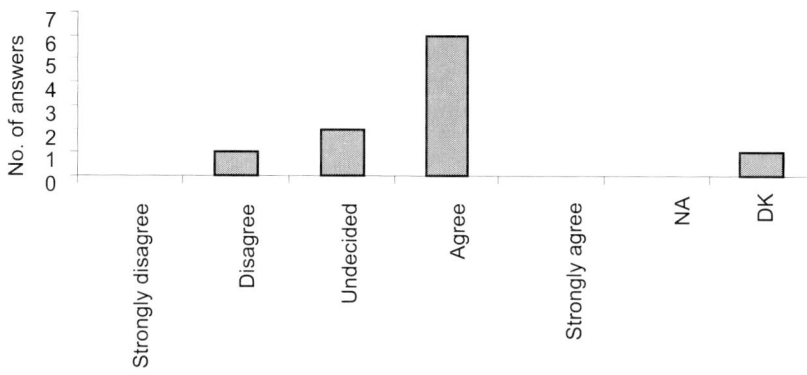

NA= not applicable; DK= do not know

Figure 11. Range of perceptions of KIs

60% agreed with the statement "Port clearing is done smoothly and there is no need for bribery or gift-giving to expedite the process" (Table 15, Figure 11).

Indicator VI.3: Is there an inspection system to verify that the medicines delivered from the port or directly from a supplier match those that were shipped from the supplier?

There is a designated staff member responsible for checking receipts against the packing list when supplies arrive at the warehouse. The responsible person should prepare documentation through a receiving report on the basis of the invoice specifying the types, quantities and condition of the supplies received.

Indicator VI.4: Is there a coding system used to identify government medicines?

Government medicines can be identified by imprints on containers and external packaging.

Indicator VI.5: Is there systematic and orderly shelving of products in warehouses or storerooms?

Products in warehouses are organized systemically by dosage forms: tablets and capsules, injections, syrups and suspensions, creams and ointments, etc. These dosage forms are arranged according to therapeutic action.

A computerized system is used to control expiry dates of medicines entered alphabetically or by manufacturer, etc.

Indicator VI.6: Is there a security management system in place to oversee storage and distribution?

There is no effective security management system to oversee storage and distribution. There are regulations for monitoring entry and exit to warehouses; to ensure limited access to unauthorized persons; and, to ensure that controlled substances (narcotics) are separated and secured. However, there is no alarm system for security breaches and there is no physical search done of those leaving the warehouse.

Indicator VI.7: Is there an inventory management system that is used in the warehouse at each level of the distribution system?

There are inventory records and procedures in the warehouses at various levels of the distribution system. The inventory control system provides information on the following elements: the average working stock; the amount of safety stock; the frequency of reordering; the quantity of reordering; the average inventory; and the lead time.

Indicator VI.8: Are stock records reconciled with physical counts at least every 3 months by internal staff?

The warehouse staff continuously produce up-to-date records of current stock levels reconciled with the physical count of selected medicines.

Indicator VI.9: Are there independent audits of warehouses by external inspectors or auditors?

The warehouses are subjected to external auditing by the Audit Bureau at regular time intervals, and random auditing by the Ministry of Health. When asked, the warehouse supervisor should be able to provide the date of the last audit that was conducted and show: a report of the warehouse audit; that the audit was carried out at least once a year; and that the audit was carried out by an independent party (Audit Bureau).

Indicator VI.10: Is there a system (computerized or manual, historical or current) in place to track the movement of pharmaceuticals from a warehouse to a health facility?

A computerized system provides information on medicines that have left the warehouse to health facilities, including: type of medicines that have left the warehouse; quantity of medicines that have left the warehouse; the person who verified the amounts; the intended recipients of these medicines; and the date that the medicines arrived at the designated health facility.

Indicator VI.11: Is there a well-functioning communication system between distribution points?

The communication system between distribution points include: a manual/document exchange system between distribution points at all levels; telephone contact between all levels of the distribution points; and fax contact between all levels of the distribution points. However, a computerized system does not exist.

Indicator VI.12: Does a programme exist for monitoring and evaluating the performance of the medicine distribution system?

There is no programme that exists for monitoring and evaluating the performance of the medicine distribution system.

Indicator VI.13: Are sanctions imposed on individuals or agencies/companies for theft or other corrupt practices associated with distribution?

Sanctions are imposed on individuals for theft or corrupt practices. There are procedures in place for the application of sanctions for corrupt behaviour. The type of sanctions to be applied depends on the nature and gravity of the act of corruption. Evidence exists that individuals have been sanctioned for corrupt behaviour in the past.

Indicator VI.14: To what extent do you agree with the following statement: "There are very rarely leakages in the medicine distribution system in your country".

50% agreed with the statement "There are very rarely leakages in the medicine distribution system in Jordan" (Table 16, Figure 12).

Indicator VI.15: If you were in a position of highest authority, what would be the first actions that you would take to improve the systems and processes of public sector medicine distribution in your country?

a) The first actions that the KIs would take to improve the systems and processes of public sector medicine distribution in Jordan in terms of the quality of services offered by the public institutions would be to:

- Train the employees of the public institution.
- Recruit ethical and qualified personnel.

Table 16. KI perceptions of the medicine distribution system

Sector	Strongly	Disagree	Undecided	Agree	Strongly	N.A.	D.K.	Total

	disagree			agree				
Government	0	2	0	4	0	0	0	6
Private	0	2	0	1	0	0	0	3
Academic	0	1	0	0	0	0	0	1
Total	0	5	0	5	0	0	0	10

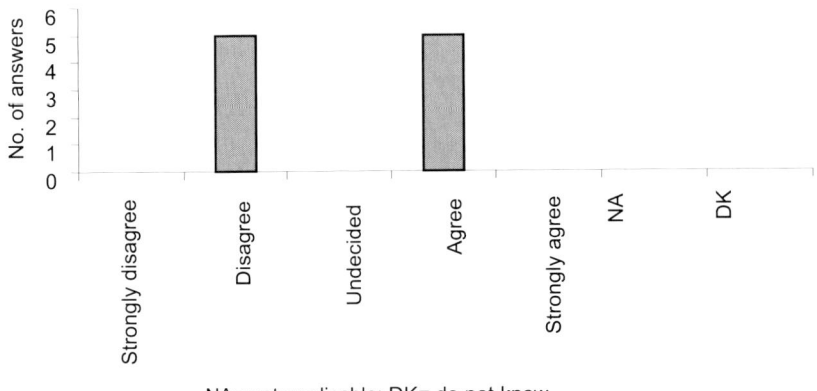

NA= not applicable; DK= do not know

Figure 12. Range of perceptions of KIs

- Introduce more effective security management to oversee storage and distribution.

- Introduce a computerized system for the communication between distribution points.

b) The first actions that the KIs would take to improve the systems and processes of public sector medicine distribution in Jordan in terms of the transparency of the services offered by the public institutions would be to:

- Submit reports identifying weakness of the distribution system and these weaknesses must be reported to the public.

5. Data analysis and interpretation

5.1 Summary

The following sections provide an area-specific analysis of the results obtained during the interviews with the key informants. It is important to stress that this information was collected during the interviews and through the analysis of the information supplied by KIs. The information is presented in the areas of registration, promotion, inspection, selection, procurements and distribution of medicines.

The study revealed that the areas of medicines registration and selection are marginally vulnerable to corruption, medicine inspection is moderately vulnerable to corruption, medicine procurement and distribution are minimally vulnerable to corruption, while medicine promotion is extremely vulnerable to corruption (Table 17 and Figure 13).

Table 17. Interpretation of results by area

Function	Score	Interpretation
Registration	7.52	Marginally vulnerable
Promotion	1.88	Extremely vulnerable
Inspection	5.79	Moderately vulnerable
Selection	7.71	Marginally vulnerable
Procurement	8.59	Minimally vulnerable
Distribution	8.41	Minimally vulnerable

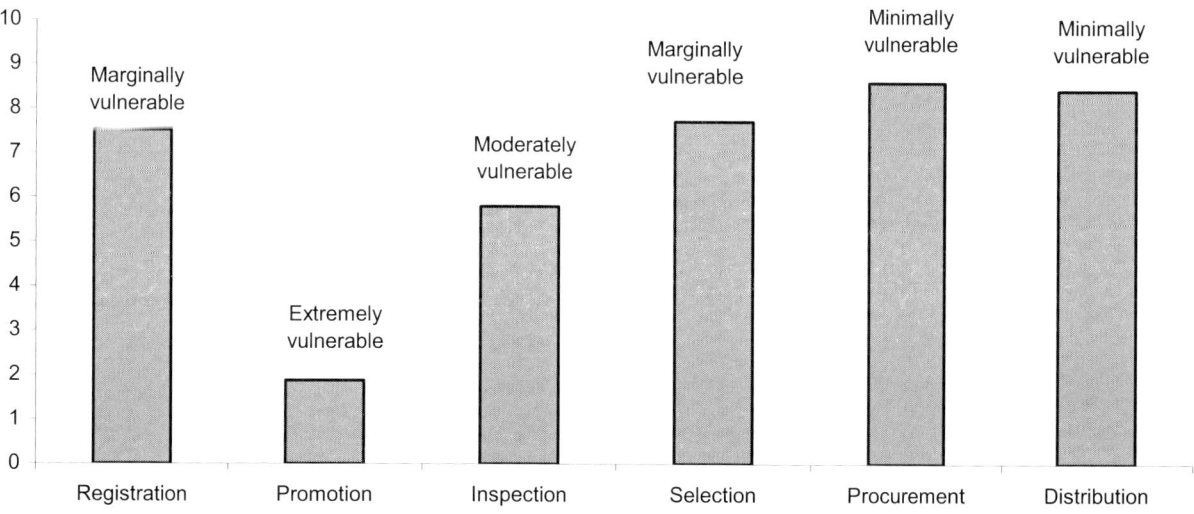

Figure 13. Vulnerability to corruption in functions of the public pharmaceutical system

5.2 Medicine registration

The decision area corresponding to medicine registration received an average indicator score of 7.52 indicating marginal vulnerability to corruption. The area of medicine registration is well documented and the requirements for the registration of new medicines are fairly well standardized. There is a fair access to information and there is an up-to-date list of all registered pharmaceutical products, which provide sufficient information about these medicines. The procedures for applicants on how to submit an application for registration of medicinal products are clearly written and publicly accessible. There is a standard application form publicly available for the submission of applications for registration of medicinal products and a formal appeals process to manage complaints from companies and medicine stores.

This area's principle weaknesses are that there are no written guidelines on conflict of interest regarding the registration activity and the members of registration committees are not required to declare any conflict of interest issues; most of the registration committees have no clear comprehensive guidelines for the committees' decision-making process; there are no clearly written or publicly accessible procedures for assessors on how to assess applications submitted for the registration of medicinal products; and finally, the criteria for selecting the members of some registration committees are not made clear enough to the public.

5.3 Control of medicine promotion

The score of 1.88 in the area of medicine promotion control indicates that this section is extremely vulnerable to corruption. This low ranking was the result of a combination of several factors. First, the provision in the medicines legislation does not cover all the activities regarding medicine promotion. Pre-approval of promotional and advertising materials is not officially required, the provision does not foresee an enforcement mechanism on promotion and advertisement of medicines, and the law does not indicate the type of sanctions or penalties to be incurred in the case of breach of the law. Second, there is no formal complaints procedure to report unethical promotional practices. Third, there is no government service or committee responsible for medicine promotion. There are no written SOPs guiding the service responsible for monitoring medicine promotion, and no written guidelines on conflict of interest. None of the KIs agreed with the statement that the legal provisions on medicine promotion have been developed in broad consultation with all interested parties, and none of them agreed with the statement that the provision on medicine promotion are well respected in Jordan. 60% of KIs agreed that civil society like Jordan Pharmaceutical Association can have a great deal of influence on improving the control of medicine promotion in Jordan.

The positive factor concerning control medicine promotion is that the Jordan Food and Drug Administration are about to issue a new regulation that will cover medicine promotion activities.

5.4 Inspections

Inspection of medicine manufacturers and distributors received a score of 5.79 indicating moderate vulnerability to corruption. There is a comprehensive provision in the medicines legislation covering the inspection of medicine manufacturers and distributors. There are written guidelines on the classification of GMP non-compliance that describe the types of deficiencies and the corresponding measures to be taken by the Medicines Regulatory Authority. There are written SOPs for inspectors on how to conduct inspection and the inspection findings and conclusions are subject to an internal review by the head of the inspection department.

That this area got the second lowest score was the result of several factors. First, there are no written guidelines on conflict of interest with regard to inspection activities. Second, there are no clear written criteria for the selection and recruitment of inspectors. Third, there are no written procedures to prevent regulatory capture between inspectors and the companies inspected. And finally, there is no external auditing of the inspection done by inspectors from another country.

5.5 Selection

The decision area corresponding to medicine selection received an average indicator score of 7.71 indicating marginal vulnerability to corruption. The first essential medicines list was published in 1998, and updated in 2002. However, in 2006, the government officially adopted the Jordan Rational Drug List (JRDL), which is available through the public health system, and helps the government to purchase appropriate medicines for their population. The government has clear guidelines that specify what criteria are applied to medicines to be included in or deleted from the JRDL. The inclusion of a new medicine should be based on studies that confirm that the medicine is necessary for the health needs of the population and is cost-effective; and, the deletion of a medicine from the JRDL is based on evidence that the medicine is inappropriate or not cost-effective for the population's health needs. However, the committee of selection does not include a member who is experienced in pharmacoeconomics.

The JRDL is available in a printed format and on the website of the JFDA[23] and so is easily accessible to all health professionals. The products are listed by generic name, pharmacological category, and by level of health care. A selection committee is appointed to give technical advice on the revision and update of the JRDL, which should be revised every 2 years. It includes physicians from different specializations and pharmacists.

This area's principle weaknesses are that there are no written guidelines on conflict of interest regarding the selection of rational medicines. The criteria for selecting committee members are not made publicly available, and the committee only includes experts from the medical and pharmacy fields. The criteria do not require members to declare issues of conflict of interest, and membership is not time-limited.

5.6 Procurement

Procurement of pharmaceuticals in public health obtained the highest rating of all six areas, earning 8.59 and thereby highlighting the high level of transparency that characterize the procedures of this area and indicating a minimal vulnerability to corruption. The government has transparent and explicit procedures that describe the procurement process for pharmaceutical products. There are written guidelines for procurement office staff on the type of procurement method to be used for different types of products, and the procurement method chosen for each product aims to obtain the lowest possible purchase price for assured quality products. A formal appeals process is available for applicants who have their bids rejected. There are clear and specific criteria for tender committee membership. The membership rotates periodically every year. There are SOPs for routine inspection of consignments and the procurement office undergoes regular external auditing through the Audit Bureau.

This area's principle weaknesses are that there are no written guidelines on conflict of interest with regard to the procurement process and the criteria for tender committee membership do not require that members declare issues of conflict of interest. Also, not all medicines procured are from the national essential medicines list (JRDL).

5.7 Distribution

The decision area corresponding to distribution of pharmaceuticals in public health received an average indicator score of 8.41 indicating minimal vulnerability to

---

[23] See: http://www.jfda.jo/RDL2/Annex/Annex.htm (accessed 5 January 2009).

corruption. The government medicines can be identified by imprints on containers and external packaging and there is systematic and orderly shelving of products in warehouses. There are inventory records and procedures in the warehouse at various levels of the distributing system and the warehouses are subjected to internal and external auditing. A computerized system provides information on medicines that have left a warehouse to health facilities. Sanctions are imposed on individuals for theft or corrupt practices.

This area's principle weaknesses are that there is no effective security management to oversee storage and distribution and there is no programme for monitoring and evaluating the performance of the medicine distribution system.

6. Recommendations

This study aimed at measuring the vulnerability of the Jordanian pharmaceutical system to corruption. Accordingly, the following recommendations attempt to address the areas where transparency is lacking within certain functions of the system. The recommendations are not tailored to address weaknesses in the system as a whole; rather, they are the sum of opinions of respondents from this assessment activity and within its scope.

Medicine registration

- Ensure the committees responsible for registration of medicines declare conflict of interest.
- Publish all requirements, process and procedures for medicine registration and SOPs and clarify the procedures of registration to the public.
- Increase the types of services offered on the JFDA website and improve the publicity of the website.
- Develop expertise and train Jordanian officials and staff on good governance and ethical practices in drug management.
- Ensure submission of files through the website. Applications should be accepted electronically, as well as the changes that occurred to the product.
- Ensure members of the appeal committee are different from those of registration committee.
- Recruit qualified personnel.
- Train the pharmacists of the registration department.
- Adopt external experts in the field of assessment.
- Enhance digital filing of administrative and technical documents.
- Increase the number of registration employees and the number of pharmacists allowed to receive applications, thus facilitating and accelerating the process of appointments.

Control of medicine promotion

- Establish a committee responsible for controlling medicine promotion with clear terms of reference, conflict of interest forms, and SOPs.
- Ensure the services offered by public institutions are clear to the public and to health professionals.
- Publish all available regulations and guidelines concerning controlling medicine promotion.
- Train health professionals on how to adopt good prescribing practice.
- Enforce a law to monitor and punish the unethical practices of medicine companies.
- Introduce a comprehensive practitioner and consumer education programme about the impact of unethical medicine promotion.

Inspections

- Post all the regulations covering the inspection of medicines, and all the guidelines and procedures regarding the inspection activity on the website.
- Put in place a clear and efficient appeal system for companies.
- Develop and publish written guidelines on conflict of interest with regard to inspection activities and mechanism of monitoring, including sanctions in case of breach of these guidelines.
- Implement a clear system for the companies' inspection schedule.
- Publish post-inspection reports.
- Provide the final report including all the inspectors' notes whenever authorized personnel from manufacturing plants request them.
- Discuss the conclusions of the inspection with the company face to face.
- Ensure the final report is signed by the company, the inspector's team and the agent.
- Train the inspectors.
- Increase the number of the inspectors.
- Ensure clear and well-defined levels of qualification and experience required for the recruitment of inspectors.
- A clear rotation mechanism for inspectors is needed.

Selection

- Publish all the scientific information pertaining to the reasons for choosing the medicines.
- Develop and enforce the standard form for conflict of interest and guidelines for the relationship between members of the medicine selection committee and pharmaceuticals.
- Change the committees of selection every year.
- Train members to review on a cost-effectiveness basis.
- Establish laws to force all doctors in the public sector to stick to the list.
- Ensure the rules for decision-making in the SOPs are clear and transparent to the public.

Procurement

- Establish written guidelines on conflict of interest with regard to the procurement process.
- Ensure the process of submission of tender is online and the results are posted on the website.
- Require members of the tender committee to declare conflict of interest.
- Include the following key functional areas in the structure of the procurement department: specification section; accountancy section; quality assurance section, including audit section; procurement section; receiving and checking section; and, information technology support.
- Restrict public sector tender procurement to the Rational Drug List.
- Review procurement procedures to ensure that prospective suppliers are pre-qualified, and their performance is monitored for product quality, service reliability, delivery time and financial viability. All information must be appropriately recorded in a retrievable database.
- Update the blacklist of non-performing or poor-performing suppliers regularly and forward a copy of the list to the procurement department.
- Simplify the procurement process to have a positive impact on the system and improve effectiveness. This can be achieved by: requiring a more evidence-based approach to medicine selection for procurement; and rationalization of medicine requirements, i.e. reducing the chemical entity in each therapeutic group, e.g. two beta blockers, two proton pump inhibitors.

Distribution

- Submit reports identifying the weakness of the distribution system and inform the public of these reports.
- Put in place more effective security management to oversee storage and distribution.
- Introduce a computerized system for communication between distribution points.

General recommendations

- Hold a national workshop with key national stakeholders to share the results of the national transparency assessment. Such a workshop could provide an opportunity for the review of the recommendations made by the national investigators. Subsequently the main elements of a national ethical framework aimed at promoting good governance for medicines regulation and procurement could be agreed upon.
- Publish the national assessment report on transparency and vulnerability to corruption, and request comments from key partners.
- Revise laws, administrative structures and procedures based on the findings of the assessment and discussions during the national workshop to ensure transparent medicines registration, promotion, inspection, selection, procurement and distribution.
- Develop a national ethics infrastructure for promoting good governance in medicines regulation and procurement through a consultation process.
- Officially, adopt the national ethics infrastructure, giving political backing to government officials to take the necessary actions to promote good governance in the pharmaceutical sector.
- Socialize the national ethical framework and the codes of conduct by training government officials to generate civil servants' sense of ownership and personal identification with an ethical framework.
- Nominate a working group that will be responsible for coordinating and managing the implementation of the Good Governance for Medicines project in the public sector, at the national level.

7. Conclusions

In the past few decades, Jordan has taken large steps towards improving its management structures for medicines. The establishment of two autonomous structures, the JFDA and the Joint Procurement Department, was a progressive step backed and supported by political leadership. These two agencies, among others, have improved the transparency of medicines governance and decreased the system's vulnerability to corruption.

Further action is still needed to improve the system. This is especially true in the area of promotion, which requires the enforcement of new regulations that cover all medicine promotion activities, and the establishment of a committee that will be responsible for controlling and monitoring medicine promotion.

In addition to continually improving the pharmaceuticals management system, effort is needed to promote a culture of transparency across the different professions in the pharmaceutical field. An ethical infrastructure document could be a useful tool to achieve this. However, such a document would need to be established in wide collaboration with various stakeholders. Even if the ethical infrastructure were initiated for the public sector, involvement of other actors who are users of the system would be beneficial to the process.

Annex 1. Scores for sections

Table A1. Medicine registration vulnerability scale point

	KI 1	KI 2	KI 3	KI 4	KI 5	KI 6	KI 7	KI 8	KI 9	KI 10	Total	Average per question
Profession	G	G	G	G	NGO	P	P	P	P	P		
Indicator I.1	1	1	1	1	1	1	1	1	1	1	10	1
Indicator I.2	1	1	0.875	1	1	1	0.875	0.875	0.875	0.875	9.375	0.9375
Indicator I.3	1	1	1	1	1	1	1	0.857	0.857	0.857	9.571	0.9571
Indicator I.4	0.833	0.5	0.5	0.5	1	0.667	0.333	0.5	0.4	0.333	5.566	0.5566
Indicator I.5	1	1	1	1	1	1	1	0.875	1	1	9.875	0.9875
Indicator I.6	1	1	1	1	1	DK	DK	1	DK	1	7	1
Indicator I.7	1	1	1	1	1	1	1	1	1	1	10	1
Indicator I.8	0.625	0.625	0.625	0.375	0.625	0.6	0.5	0.625	0.85	0.5	5.95	0.595
Indicator I.9	0.75	0.75	0.75	0.625	0.625	0.6	0.714	0.571	0.333	0.5	6.218	0.6218
Indicator I.10	0	0	0	0	0	0	0	0	0	0	0	0
Indicator I.12	0.857	0.571	0.286	0.571	0.286	0	0.25	0.6	0	0.286	3.707	0.3707
Indicator I.13	1	1	1	1	1	1	1	1	1	1	10	1
											Total	9.0262
											Final score	7.52

Table A2. Medicine promotion control vulnerability scale points

	KI 1	KI 2	KI 3	KI 4	KI 5	KI 6	KI 7	KI 8	KI 9	KI 10	Total	Average per question
Profession	NGO	G	O	O	O	P	P	P	P	P		
Indicator II.1	1	1	1	1	0	1	1	1	1	1	9	0.9
Indicator II.2	0.5	0.5	0.5	0.2	0	0.5	0.4	0.5	0.4	0.5	4	0.4
Indicator II.3	0	0	0	0	0	0	0	0	0	0	0	0
Indicator II.4	0	0	1	0	0	1	0	0	0	0	2	0.2
Indicator II.5	0	0	0	0	0	0	0	0	0	0	0	0
Indicator II.6	0	0	0	0	0	0	0	0	0	0	0	0
Indicator II.7	0	0	0	0	0	0	0	0	0	0	0	0
Indicator II.8	0	0	0	0	0	0	0	0	0	0	0	0
											Total	1.5
											Final score	1.88

Table A3. Medicine inspection vulnerability scale point

	KI 1	KI 2	KI 3	KI 4	KI 5	KI 6	KI 7	KI 8	KI 9	KI 10	Total	Average per question
Profession	G	G	G	G	O	P	P	P	P	P		
Indicator III.1	1	1	1	1	1	1	1	1	1	1	10	1
Indicator III.2	1	1	1	1	0.75	0.5	0.25	0.75	1	1	8.25	0.825
Indicator III.3	0.833	0.5	0.5	0.5	0.5	0.667	0.167	0.8	0.667	0.5	5.634	0.5634
Indicator III.4	0.833	0.667	0.167	0.5	0	0	0.5	0	0.5	0.33	3.497	0.3497
Indicator III.5	0	0	0	0	0	0	0	0	0	0	0	0
Indicator III.6	1	1	1	1	1	1	1	1	1	1	10	1
Indicator III.7	1	1	0.8	1	0.2	1	0	0.6	1	0.8	7.4	0.74
Indicator III.8	0.25	0.75	0	0.25	0	0	0	0	0.25	0	1.5	0.15
											Total	4.6281
											Final score	5.79

Table A4. Medicine selection vulnerability scale points

	KI 1	KI 2	KI 3	KI 4	KI 5	KI 6	KI 7	KI 8	KI 9	KI 10	Total	Average per question
Profession	G	G	G	G	G	G	G	O	P	NGO		
Indicator IV.1	1	1	1	1	1	1	1	1	1	1	10	1
Indicator IV.3	1	0.857	0.833	1	1	0.857	1	0.857	0.8	1	9.204	0.9204
Indicator IV.4	1	0.833	0.833	0.833	1	0.833	0.833	0.8	0.667	0.833	8.465	0.8465
Indicator IV.5	1	1	1	1	1	1	1	1	1	1	10	1
Indicator IV.7	0.571	0.429	0.571	0.571	0.571	0.571	0.667	0.5	0.286	0.571	5.308	0.5308
Indicator IV.8	0	0	0	0	0	0	0	0	0	0	0	0
Indicator IV.9	1	1	1	1	1	1	1	1	1	1	10	1
Indicator IV.10	1	0.8	1	0.833	1	0.833	0.833	0.8	0.75	0.833	8.682	0.8682
											Total	6.1659
											Final score	7.71

Table A5. Medicine procurement vulnerability scale points

	KI 1	KI 2	KI 3	KI 4	KI 5	KI 6	KI 7	KI 8	KI 9	KI 10	KI 11	Total	Average per question
Profession*	G	G	G	G	G	G	G	O	G	P	O		
Indicator V.1	1	0.889	0.889	0.889	0.889	1	1	0.889	1	0.875	0.889	10.209	0.928
Indicator V.2	1	1	1	1	1	1	1	D.K.	1	1	1	10	1
Indicator V.3	1	1	1	D.K.	1	1	1	1	1	1	1	10	1
Indicator V.4	1	1	1	1	1	1	1	1	1	1	1	11	1
Indicator V.5	1	1	1	1	1	1	1	1	1	1	1	11	1
Indicator V.6	0.714	0.571	0.714	0.4	0.571	0.714	0.571	0.5	0.5	0.5	0.571	6.326	0.575
Indicator V.7	0	0	0	0	0	0	0	0	0	0	0	0	0
Indicator V.9	1	1	1	1	1	1	1	1	1	1	1	11	1
Indicator V.10	1	1	1	1	1	1	1	1	1	1	1	11	1
Indicator V.11	1	1	1	1	0.667	1	1	1	1	1	1	10.667	0.969
Indicator V.12	1	1	0.875	1	1	1	1	1	1	1	0.875	10.75	0.977
											Total		9.450
											Final score		8.59

Table A6. Medicine distribution vulnerability scale points

	KI 1	KI 2	KI 3	KI 4	KI 5	KI 6	KI 7	KI 8	KI 9	KI 10	Total	Average per question
Profession	G	G	G	G	G	G	O	P	P	P		
Indicator VI.1	1	1	1	1	1	1	1	1	1	1	10	1
Indicator VI.3	1	1	1	1	1	1	1	1	1	1	10	1
Indicator VI.4	1	1	1	1	1	1	1	1	1	1	10	1
Indicator VI.5	1	1	1	1	1	1	1	1	1	1	10	1
Indicator VI.6	0.5	0.25	0.5	0.5	0.333	0.333	0.333	0.5	0.5	0	3.749	0.3749
Indicator VI.7	1	1	1	1	1	1	1	1	1	1	10	1
Indicator VI.8	1	1	1	1	1	1	1	1	1	1	10	1
Indicator VI.9	1	1	1	1	1	1	1	1	1	1	10	1
Indicator VI.10	1	1	1	1	1	1	1	1	1	0.833	9.833	0.9833
Indicator VI.11	0.75	0.75	0.75	0.5	0.75	0.75	0.75	0.75	0.75	0.75	7.25	0.725
Indicator VI.12	0	0.143	0	0	0	0	0	0	0	0	0.143	0.0143
Indicator VI.13	1	1	1	1	1	1	1	1	1	1	10	1
											Total	10.0975
											Final score	8.41

Table A7. Total areas vulnerability scale points

Area	Total indicators	Number of key informants	Score on 10 point scale	Degree of vulnerability to corruption
Registration	16	10	7.52	Marginally
Promotion	12	10	1.88	Extremely
Inspection	11	10	5.79	Moderately
Selection	12	10	7.71	Marginally
Procurement	15	11	8.59	Minimally
Distribution	15	10	8.41	Minimally
Total	**66**	**61**	**6.65**	**Marginally**

Annex 2. Ministry of Health organizational chart

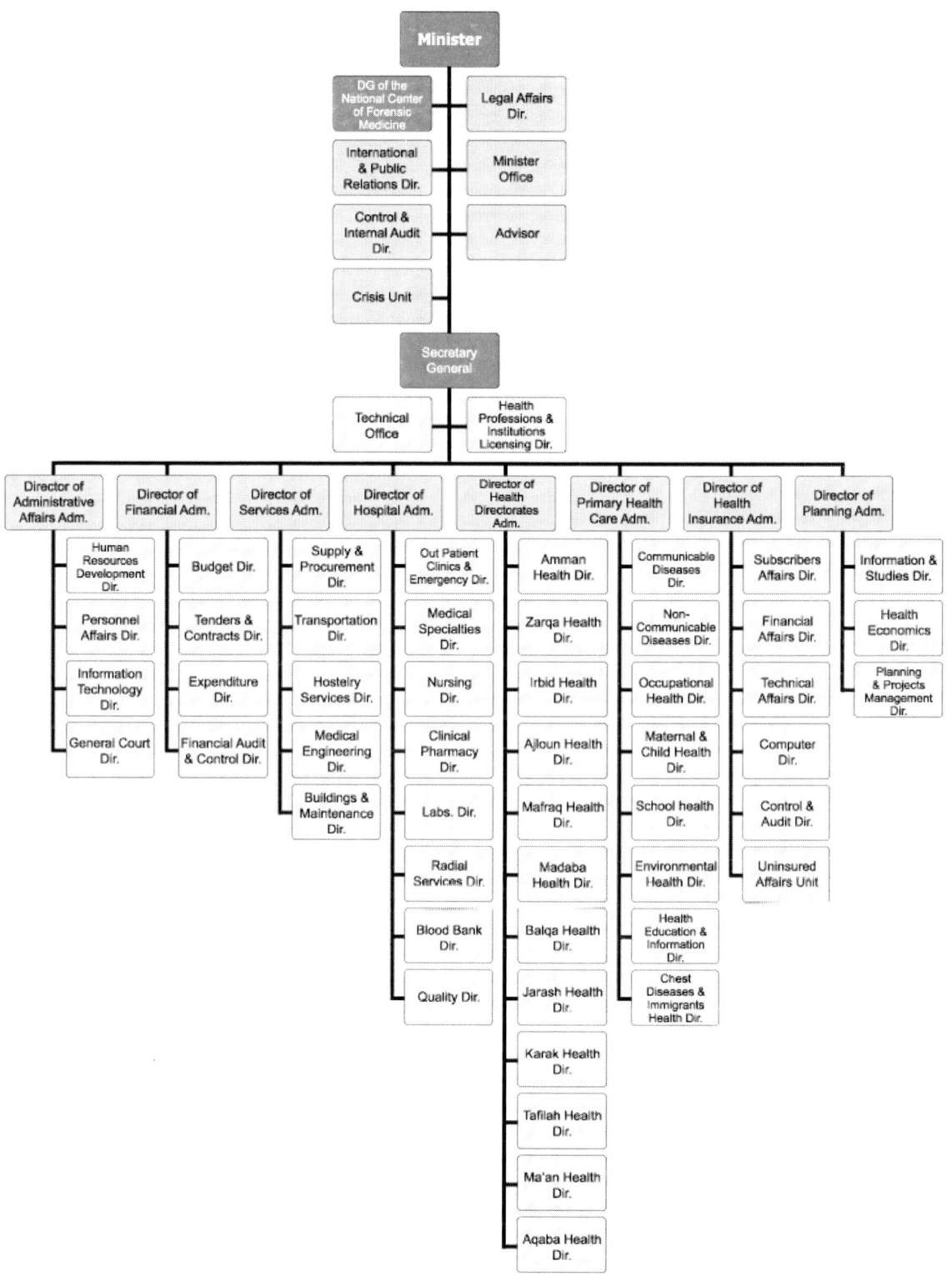

Annex 3. Jordan Food and Drug Administration organizational chart

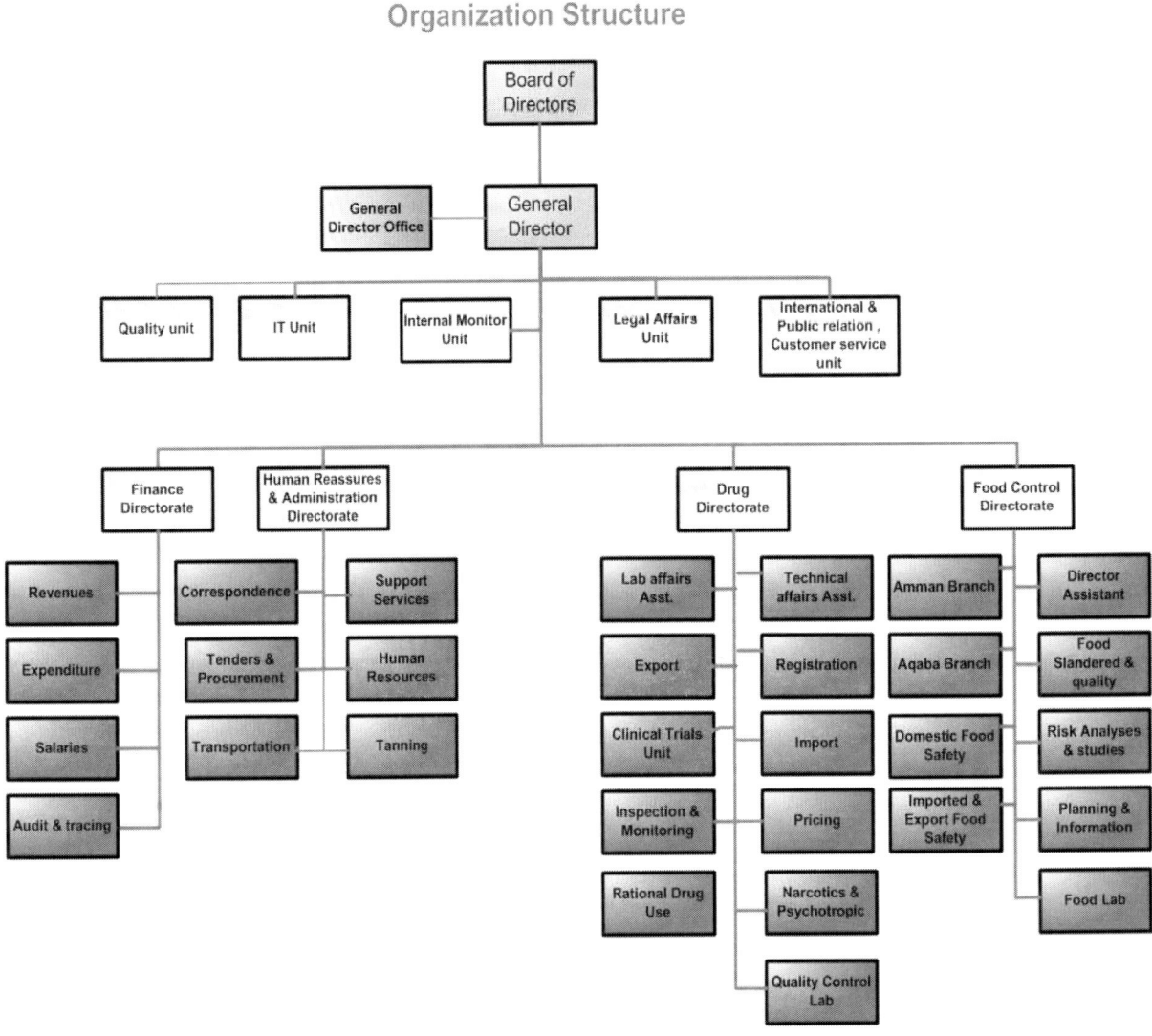

Annex 4. Joint Procurement Department organizational chart

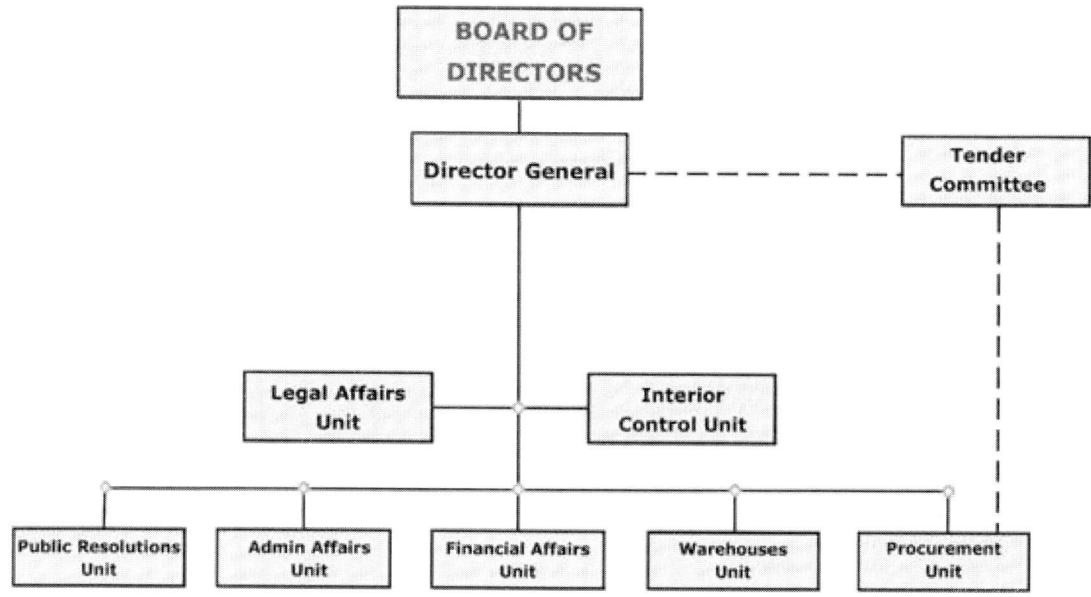

Annex 5. List of evidence obtained

The following documents were gathered from the JFDA website and relevant departments within the JFDA and Ministry of Health.

1. Drug and Pharmacy Law of 2001.
2. Joint Procurement Law of Medicines and Medical Supplies.
3. An up-to-date list of all registered pharmaceutical products.
4. Written procedures for applicants on how to submit an application for registration of medicinal products
5. A standard application form publicly available for the submission of applications for registration of medicinal products.
6. Written criteria for selecting the committees members for the registration of originators and generic drugs and the term of reference of these committees
7. Provision in the medicines legislation that mention drug promotion and advertising.
8. Provision in the medicines legislation/regulation covering inspection of medicines manufacturers and distributors.
9. Written guidelines on the classification of Good Manufacturing Practices (GMP) that describe the types of deficiencies and the corresponding measures to be taken by the Medicines Regulatory Authority.
10. Written SOPs for inspectors on how to conduct inspections.
11. Rational Drug List that the government have a officially adopted and, which is publicly available
12. Written SOPs that describe the rules for the decision making process regardaddition or deletion of medicines from the Rational Drug List.
13. Written criteria for including or deleting medicines from the Rational Drug List.
14. A document that describes the procurement process for the pharmaceutical product.
15. Written criteria for tender committee membership.